CLASSICS IN EDUCATION
Lawrence A. Cremin, General Editor

☆ ☆ ☆

THE REPUBLIC AND THE SCHOOL
Horace Mann on the Education of Free Men
Edited by Lawrence A. Cremin

AMERICAN IDEAS ABOUT ADULT EDUCATION
1710–1951
Edited by C. Hartley Grattan

DEWEY ON EDUCATION
Introduction and Notes by Martin S. Dworkin

THE SUPREME COURT AND EDUCATION
Edited by David Fellman

INTERNATIONAL EDUCATION
A Documentary History
Edited by David G. Scanlon

CRUSADE AGAINST IGNORANCE
Thomas Jefferson on Education
Edited by Gordon C. Lee

CHINESE EDUCATION UNDER COMMUNISM
Edited by Chang-tu Hu

CHARLES W. ELIOT AND POPULAR EDUCATION
Edited by Edward A. Krug

WILLIAM T. HARRIS ON EDUCATION
(in preparation)
Edited by Martin S. Dworkin

THE *EMILE* OF JEAN JACQUES ROUSSEAU
Selections
Translated and Edited by William Boyd

THE MINOR EDUCATIONAL WRITINGS OF
JEAN JACQUES ROUSSEAU
Selected and Translated by William Boyd

PSYCHOLOGY AND THE SCIENCE OF EDUCATION
Selected Writings of Edward L. Thorndike
Edited by Geraldine M. Joncich

THE NEW-ENGLAND PRIMER
Introduction by Paul Leicester Ford

BENJAMIN FRANKLIN ON EDUCATION
Edited by John Hardin Best

THE COLLEGES AND THE PUBLIC
1787–1862
Edited by Theodore Rawson Crane

TRADITIONS OF AFRICAN EDUCATION
Edited by David G. Scanlon

NOAH WEBSTER'S AMERICAN SPELLING BOOK
Introductory Essay by Henry Steele Commager

VITTORINO DA FELTRE
AND OTHER HUMANIST EDUCATORS
by William Harrison Woodward
Foreword by Eugene F. Rice, Jr.

DESIDERIUS ERASMUS
CONCERNING THE AIM AND METHOD
OF EDUCATION
By William Harrison Woodward
Foreword by Craig R. Thompson

JOHN LOCKE ON EDUCATION
Edited by Peter Gay

CATHOLIC EDUCATION IN AMERICA
A Documentary History
Edited by Neil G. McCluskey, S.J.

THE AGE OF THE ACADEMIES
Edited by Theodore R. Sizer

HEALTH, GROWTH, AND HEREDITY
G. Stanley Hall on Natural Education
Edited by Charles E. Strickland and Charles Burgess

TEACHER EDUCATION IN AMERICA
A Documentary History
Edited by Merle L. Borrowman

THE EDUCATED WOMAN IN AMERICA
Selected Writings of Catharine Beecher,
Margaret Fuller, and M. Carey Thomas
Edited by Barbara M. Cross

EMERSON ON EDUCATION
Selections
Edited by Howard Mumford Jones

ECONOMIC INFLUENCES UPON EDUCATIONAL PROGRESS IN THE UNITED STATES, 1820–1850
By Frank Tracy Carlton
Foreword by Lawrence A. Cremin

Economic Influences upon Educational Progress in the United States, 1820–1850

By FRANK TRACY CARLTON

With a Foreword by
LAWRENCE A. CREMIN

TEACHERS COLLEGE PRESS
TEACHERS COLLEGE, COLUMBIA UNIVERSITY
NEW YORK

Library of Congress Catalog Card
Number 66–11657

Original edition published 1908
by the University of Wisconsin

Printed in the United States of America
by the William Byrd Press, Inc.
Richmond, Virginia

Contents

Foreword

By LAWRENCE A. CREMIN

The social sciences were enjoying something of a golden age at the University of Wisconsin when Frank Tracy Carlton arrived there in 1904 to take up his recently won fellowship in economics. President Charles Van Hise had just assumed office on a platform of applying the fruits of systematic research to the rational solution of social problems; and the School of Economics and Politics, under the energetic leadership of Richard T. Ely, was already producing a steady flow of relevant materials. Ely himself had literally created the field of labor economics and, with his young associate, Thomas Sewall Adams, was publishing a brilliant succession of books, pamphlets, and articles. William A. Scott was undertaking his pioneering investigations into the problems of public finance; Paul Reinsch was pressing forward his incisive inquiries into the politics of colonialism; and John R. Commons, who had only recently come from New York, was initiating the studies that would culminate in the *Documentary History of American Industrial Society* (1910–1911) and the *History of Labour in the United States* (1918–1935).[1] The work was imaginative, stimulating, and suffused with a spirit of reform. "I

[1] See Merle Curti and Vernon Carstensen, *The University of Wisconsin: A History, 1848–1925* (2 vols.; Madison, Wis.: University of Wisconsin Press, 1949).

was guided," Ely later reminisced, "by the wish that the training which the ever-growing numbers of young people received at Wisconsin would enable them to contribute directly to human progress. I was, and am, an optimist and a believer in progress."[2]

Carlton, who at thirty was somewhat older than the average university student, came determined to make the most of the opportunity. Born and educated in Ohio, he had attended the Case Institute in Cleveland (B.S., 1895; M.E., 1899) and had then taught for a time at the Toledo University Manual Training School. It was with the idea of preparing himself as a professor of physics that he had enrolled for summer work at the University of Michigan and at Cornell; and it was at Cornell, in 1901, that he had abruptly changed his plans.[3] As Carlton later related it, he was listening one morning to the first few minutes of an inordinately dull physics lecture when he decided, on the spur of the moment, to slip into a nearby economics class and "see what it was like."[4] He found himself fascinated and promptly abandoned the study of physics for the study of economics. There was further work at the University of Chicago during the summers of 1902 and 1903;[5] and then, in 1904, he won the fellowship at Wisconsin.

[2] Richard T. Ely, *Ground under Our Feet* (New York: The Macmillan Co., 1938), p. 185.

[3] The biographical data on Carlton (1873–1961) are from a vita in the archives of the Case Institute of Technology.

[4] A. P. Fraas, "Faculty Portraits: Dr. Frank T. Carlton, '95," *Case Alumnus,* May 17, 1938, p. 46.

[5] Carlton's record at the University of Chicago, which was made available to me by Richard J. Storr, reveals that he completed six courses in political economy, three in sociology, and one in political science. Of these, the most significant with respect to his doctoral thesis would appear to have been "Economics of Workingmen," with John Cummings, and "A Synopsis of Sociological Theory," with Albion Small. (Actually, there are minor discrepancies between the

We have few records of the two years Carlton spent in Madison. He apparently worked under Ely, taking eight courses with the master himself, four with Adams, four with Reinsch, two with Scott, and one with Commons.[6] One can only guess at how he happened upon his dissertation topic, though it is probable that the initial suggestion came from Ely, who had dealt with education in *The Labor Movement in America* (1886) and who was beginning, with Commons, to assign topics in connection with the projected *Documentary History*. In any case, by 1905 Carlton was well launched on his study; in 1906 he completed his work for the doctorate and won a professorship at Albion College; and in 1908 the dissertation was published under the title *Economic Influences upon Educational Progress in the United States, 1820–1850*.

Carlton's theses were forthrightly presented, extensively documented, and strikingly original. For more than a generation, students of education had explained the "educational revival" of the early nineteenth century as the work of a few great and dedicated humanitarians, men such as Henry Barnard, James G. Carter, Samuel Lewis, and Horace Mann, who had awakened the public to the need for universal education and led in the effort to disseminate New England's common-school ideals through the nation at large. Carlton, on the other hand, saw the educational revival as but one phase of a larger social development, contending that (1) "the tax-supported school system evolved out of heterogeneity of population, improvement in methods of production, the

---

listings on Carlton's record and those in the University of Chicago *Annual Register* for 1901–1902 and 1902–1903.)

[6] Carlton's record at the University of Wisconsin was made available to me by Vernon Carstensen.

specialization of industry, the division of labor, the growth of factories and the separation of home life from industrial occupations"; (2) the public school system was "the resultant of the conflict of interests—economic, social, religious and racial—within the different states"; and (3) "the cities and the working classes were chiefly instrumental in placing our schools upon a tax-supported basis." With respect to public policy for his own time, Carlton drew a clear moral: social forces, not altruistic leaders, had been and would continue to be the decisive factors in American educational progress. "If generalization is warranted by the data before us," he counseled, "the conclusion is warranted that, in modern times, the trend of educational advance is determined by economic evolution. On the one hand, the student of educational problems, who is striving to improve the work of the public schools, must study the trend of industrial and social evolution; and, on the other hand, the political economist and social scientist must consider the economic and social significance of uniform advance in educational and industrial evolution."

For all its boldness and originality, Carlton's monograph elicited surprisingly little comment when it first appeared. *The Annals of the American Academy of Political and Social Science* carried a brief summary, and *The School Review* gave it passing mention in connection with an appraisal of another of Carlton's books issued the same year.[7] But one searches the learned journals in vain for any further notice of its publication. Per-

[7] *The Annals of the American Academy of Political and Social Science,* XXXIII (1909), 713–714, and *The School Review,* XVII (1909), 726–727. The other book Carlton published in 1908 was *Education and Industrial Evolution;* it was widely and favorably reviewed, and remains valuable as a characteristic Progressive tract on education.

haps the most interesting response came in a letter from Max Farrand of Yale. "My first impressions were rather unfavorable," he wrote to Carlton early in 1910, "for I thought you were using too much secondary material, but gradually your point of view unfolded itself and I began to appreciate the larger view which you were taking. Some of your ideas are too new for me to be sure as yet that I can accept them, but they are certainly big ideas and suggest many possibilities."[8]

Despite the paucity of scholarly notice, however, Carlton's theses were destined to exert profound influence. In 1910, for example, John R. Commons and Helen L. Sumner gave them unqualified endorsement in the monumental *Documentary History of American Industrial Society*. "Hitherto," they wrote, "our historical knowledge of the free-school movement has ascribed that movement to the great humanitarian leaders with Horace Mann at their head. But Mr. Carlton, after a careful study of the documents herewith presented, concludes that 'the vitality of the movement for tax-supported schools was derived, not from the humanitarian leaders, but from the growing class of wage-earners.' The working men placed this demand foremost. The older parties took it up and candidates pledged themselves to it. The educational leaders appealed to a constituency already awakened. The Working Men's Party disappeared, but its issue was adopted by all parties, and free education became the finest fruit of universal suffrage."[9] Eight years later, this endorsement was repeated in the first volume

[8] Max Farrand to Frank Tracy Carlton, January 4, 1910. The letter is in the archives of the Case Institute of Technology.

[9] John R. Commons *et al.*, eds., *A Documentary History of American Industrial Society* (10 vols.; Cleveland: The Arthur H. Clark Co., 1910–1911), V, 27–28.

of the *History of Labour in the United States,* which quickly became the standard work in its field.[10] Carlton himself restated his theses in *Organized Labor in American History* (1920), which was to be his magnum opus; and so far as can be determined, he continued to support them throughout his extraordinarily long and productive career.[11]

As in labor history, so also in educational history. In 1909, Ellwood P. Cubberley's *Changing Conceptions of Education* appeared, bearing patent evidence of Carlton's influence. Ten years later, with the publication of Cubberley's *Public Education in the United States,* it became clear that Carlton's influence had been decisive, not only with respect to periodization, but also in the conceptualization of the seven celebrated "battles" for the free public school system (though Cubberley did make much less of any special contribution by the workingmen).[12] And given the dominance of Cubberley's formulations in the teaching and writing of American educational history over the succeeding quarter-century, it is probably fair to suggest that, through him, Carlton's ideas significantly affected a whole generation of American educators.

Carlton's ideas also found their way into a number of later works, though in substantially modified form. Thus,

[10] John R. Commons *et al., History of Labour in the United States* (4 vols.; New York: The Macmillan Co., 1918–1935), I, 223–230, 246–260.

[11] Carlton remained at Albion College until 1919, when he accepted a professorship of economics at DePauw University. Eight years later, he returned to his alma mater to head a new department of economics; and though he became professor emeritus in 1950, he continued to teach and write until his death in 1961.

[12] See my essay *The Wonderful World of Ellwood Patterson Cubberley* (New York: Bureau of Publications, Teachers College, Columbia University, 1965).

for example, my own book, *The American Common School* (1951), dealt at length with the contributions of Robert Dale Owen and other labor publicists, though it did regard these contributions as essentially ancillary to those of the humanitarian reformers. And Rush Welter's *Popular Education and Democratic Thought in America* (1962) also assigned a central place to the campaign of the workingmen but emphasized consensus rather than conflict as the key to the politics of pre-Civil War education. My current view is that both Welter's book and mine tended to overstate labor's influence in the educational movement of the 1830's and 1840's.

Needless to say, there has been criticism of Carlton's work over the years, addressed chiefly to his assertions concerning labor's special role in the establishment of the public school. In 1926, for example, Philip R. V. Curoe published *Educational Attitudes and Policies of Organized Labor in the United States,* in which he documented a long record of labor support for public education but took issue with one of Carlton's principal arguments. "In the two decades preceding the Civil War," Curoe noted, "the points of contact between our educational development and organized labor were neither many nor important. Labor's concerns were either with comprehensive schemes of social regeneration—the most notable of which was Fourierism—or with strictly economic policies. . . . On the whole, the labor organizations of the period furnished little of the 'drive' which was needed to bring to realization the progressive program of Horace Mann and other educational leaders of this time."[13] Similar reservations were advanced by Sid-

[13] Philip R. V. Curoe, *Educational Attitudes and Policies of Organized Labor in the United States* (New York: Bureau of Publications, Teachers College, Columbia University, 1926), p. 191.

ney L. Jackson, who contended in *America's Struggle for Free Schools* (1941) that while urban craftsmen had contributed significantly to the common-school revival, insufficient attention had been given to the role of other social groups, notably, middle-class intellectuals and the clergy.[14] With the publication of Arthur M. Schlesinger, Jr.'s, *The Age of Jackson* in 1945, and the spate of reactions and rejoinders it stimulated, the criticism sharpened, revolving largely around questions concerning the character of the Jacksonian wage earner and the nature of his organizations and programs. And in 1964 Jay Marvin Pawa undertook a full-scale review of Carlton's theses in a doctoral study at Columbia, concluding that Carlton was quite in error about the role of labor and that the public school revival of the early nineteenth century was far more a middle-class than a working-class phenomenon.[15] One can raise questions about Pawa's definition of labor, just as Pawa did about Carlton's and Curoe's. Nevertheless, Pawa's arguments, at least on the basis of evidence from New York State, appear to be well grounded.

Despite these criticisms, Carlton's treatise still deserves serious study. It was seminal in its own time, and it remains exceedingly suggestive today. One can repudiate its rather crude economic determinism and still be in-

[14] Sidney L. Jackson, *America's Struggle for Free Schools* (Washington, D.C.: American Council on Public Affairs, 1941), pp. 172–173. See also Jackson, "Labor, Education, and Politics in the 1830's," *The Pennsylvania Magazine of History and Biography*, LXVI (1942), 279.

[15] Jay Marvin Pawa, "The Attitude of Labor Organizations in New York State toward Public Education, 1829–1890" (Unpublished doctoral thesis, Teachers College, Columbia University, 1964). Chapter 1 of Pawa's study is a useful critical review of the relevant literature. See also Charles Grier Sellers, Jr., *Jacksonian Democracy* (Washington, D.C.: Service Center for Teachers of History, 1958).

structed by its insistence on the classical inseparability of education and politics. One can criticize its somewhat narrow pro-labor bias and still be persuaded that self-interest is at least as significant as altruism in the development of reform movements. And one can reject the naïveté of its political analysis and still agree that such analysis is indispensable to an understanding of the rise of the public school.

Ultimately, what Carlton did was to offer the model for a serious political and economic history of American education at a time when the standard texts were portraying the public school as a gift sprung full-blown from the heads of the Puritan fathers. That political and economic history has yet to be written, though we have illustrations of how it might look in the work of Hendrik D. Gideonse on antebellum Connecticut, Forrest David Mathews on antebellum Georgia and Alabama, Lloyd P. Jorgenson on antebellum Wisconsin, Jonathan C. Messerli on antebellum Massachusetts, and Daniel H. Calhoun and Julia Duffy on antebellum New York.[16] The generalizations issuing from this research have been cautiously advanced and hedged with all sorts of qualifications; nevertheless, they do tend to challenge Carlton's theses concerning the special role of the workingmen. Yet the value of Carlton's work is by no means diminished;

[16] Hendrik D. Gideonse, "Common School Reform: Connecticut, 1838–1854" (Unpublished doctoral thesis, Graduate School of Education, Harvard University, 1963); Forrest David Mathews, "The Politics of Education in the Deep South: Georgia and Alabama, 1830–1860" (Unpublished doctoral thesis, Teachers College, Columbia University, 1965); Lloyd P. Jorgenson, *The Founding of Public Education in Wisconsin* (Madison, Wis.: State Historical Society of Wisconsin, 1956); and Jonathan C. Messerli, "Horace Mann: The Early Years, 1796–1837" (Unpublished doctoral thesis, Harvard University, 1963). The work of Professor Calhoun at Harvard and Miss Duffy at Columbia is in progress.

for it is the questions he asked rather than the answers he ventured that were his most fundamental contribution and that constitute his continuing legacy to students of American educational history.

Economic Influences upon Educational Progress in the United States, 1820–1850

A NOTE ON THE TEXT

This volume has been reset from the *Bulletin of the University of Wisconsin,* No. 221, Economics and Political Science Series, Vol. IV, No. 1, pp. 1–135. Unfortunately, Carlton was somewhat casual about matters of punctuation, abbreviation, and orthography, and one finds blatant inconsistencies in his usage and style. Nevertheless, it has seemed wise to reprint his monograph with no changes in text or documentation, and to confine the use of *"sic"* to his most egregious spelling errors.

Introduction*

The nineteenth century witnessed a revolutionary transformation in education as well as in economic and social conditions. Writers on educational development have almost uniformly adhered to the "great man" theory; few attempts have been made to trace the relation between educational advance and industrial progress. Economists have devoted much energy to the study of tariff and financial history, of the development of labor unions, of socialism and of other industrial, political and social phenomena connected with the progress of the nation. But the evolution of the public school system —one of the most characteristic institutions of the United States—has not been carefully studied with the aim of bringing to light the underlying social and economic influences which have directed it. Nevertheless, the character of education—its aims, ideals, methods, values, scope and diffusion—is an important factor in fixing the economic and social conditions of a given people and generation, and in influencing the future development of a nation.

The scope of education in the centuries preceding the nineteenth was very narrow. The development of the factory system and the growth of modern cities, accompanied by great changes in the manner of living and of working, have given the school new problems,—problems which formerly devolved upon the home and the

* Acknowledgment is made of assistance received from the American Bureau of Industrial Research in the preparation of this study.

workshop. The functions of an educational system depend upon the civilization of the people using that system, and upon the progress of the arts and sciences, in short, upon the economic and social conditions.[1] In a primitive society the duties of the school were few; in a complex industrial society, having crowded population centers, practicing division of labor and specialization of industry, its functions become varied and important. The history of education should be an orderly account of the varying educational needs, and of the progressive and conservative forces which mold the educational institutions of different historic periods. Three and possibly four, epochs may be distinguished in our educational progress. The last three are practically contemporaneous with periods of rapid economic and social change. Between these epochs are intervals of slow educational advance or of retrogression. Educational evolution, like industrial and social progress, is not uniform, but irregular; it advances now rapidly, now slowly. In the early Colonial period, education was advocated mainly by the Calvinistic clergy, and for religious reasons. The second epoch extends approximately from 1820 to 1850. Education was then urged on civic, economic and ethical grounds. During this period occurred the struggle for free tax-supported schools; and during the period the school became secular in character. In the third period (1875–1890) the industrial and psychological value of education was placed in the foreground; and the curriculum was rapidly expanded. At the threshold of the fourth epoch (1900–) education begins to assume a paternalistic attitude. Sociological considerations now

[1] The writer, *The Influence of Recent Economic and Social Changes upon Educational Aims, Ideals and Methods* in *Journal of Pedagogy*, March, 1906.

take an important place in pedagogical discussions. The school is assuming many new functions which were hitherto performed by the home.[2]

Perhaps the most important contribution of the American people to educational advance is the general establishment of a tax-supported school system free for all children. It is our present task to study the period which established beyond controversy, in the United States, this important educational principle. In this period many agitations and reform movements sprang into being and flourished for a time. Are all these divergent agitations and reform movements isolated and disconnected phenomena? Are these manifestations the results, solely or in most part, of the patient and arduous labors of scores of able and devoted men? Or have these movements some underlying, semi-hidden cause or causes? The task before us is to study and weigh the forces, direct and indirect, which led to the so-called "educational revival" of 1820 to 1850.

[2] See article by the writer, *The Home and the School* in *Education,* December, 1905.

1. The Colonial Period

In a progressive age institutions,—legal, political, social and educational,—always lag behind economic progress. This is the normal result due to the action of reactionary or conservative forces, called precedent, which are crystallized into law, custom and sentiment. In order to understand the progress of education, the modifications in its methods, aims and values, it is necessary to consider not only the changing social, economic and political conditions during our special period, but also to roughly survey the preceding period in which are found the roots of the later vigorous growth, or, in other words, the modifying and restraining influences which bear upon progress during the later epoch.

The influence of New England was very marked throughout the entire westward movement of population. New England men became leaders, and carried with them and impressed upon the various new communities, New England customs, manners, religious beliefs and educational methods. Imitation played a considerable role in the development of the West. The other settlers were dominated and influenced by the strong, individualistic man from New England, and were soon found adopting the customs and ideals of the latter. On account of this fact, if for no other reason, the attention may during the study of the early period of our history, be directed chiefly to New England.

The roots of the free school movement may be easily

traced back to Luther and the Reformation.[1] Luther advocated compulsory education for all children, exactly as military service was made compulsory. "One of the cardinal requirements of democratic Calvinism has always been elementary education for everybody. In matters of religion all souls are equally concerned and each individual is ultimately responsible for himself. The Scriptures are the rule of life, and accordingly each individual ought to be able to read them for himself, without dependence upon priests. Hence it is one of the prime duties of a congregation to insist that all members shall know how to read and, if necessary, to provide them with the requisite instruction." In accordance with this Calvinistic idea some form of universal and compulsory elementary education sprang up during the 16th and 17th centuries wherever Calvinism had become dominant,—in the Protestant parts of France and Switzerland, in Holland, in the Netherlands, and in New England.[2] This relation between religion and education is important, and furnishes the key to an understanding of our early educational development. The decadence of education during the later part of the 18th and the early portion of the 19th centuries was a necessary and inevitable accompaniment of the weakening and the final severance of the ties which bound the two together. The so-called educational revival of the second quarter of the 19th century is the result of the alliance of education with new forces.

With the possible exception of Holland, it must be noted that the early schools which were the product of Calvinism was middle-class schools, rather than schools for the masses. In England, from the middle of the 16th

[1] Perrin, J. W., *Compulsory Education,* 5.

[2] Fiske, *The Dutch and Quaker Colonies in America,* 1:33.

to well into the 17th century, a powerful educational movement manifested itself in the establishment of various kinds of schools, especially grammar schools. By the beginning of the 18th century, England was by no means poorly supplied with grammar schools, while there were many schools of a lower grade, either free English schools or charity schools.[3] In Scotland, John Knox did draw up a comprehensive scheme of education; and an Act was passed which embodied many of its features. The law was, however, repealed a few years later at the time of the Restoration.[4] In Holland the leading class was composed of merchants, and elementary education was valued as a training for a trading career.[5]

The early New England men who exerted such a powerful influence upon the development of the northern and western portions of the United States were drawn from the flower of a fine class of English rural gentry and yeomen.[6] They came to the New World in order to avoid persecution and oppression. They brought with them English law, customs, traditions and form of local government; but under the modifying influence of a new environment and by reason of friction with the mother country, they modified many customs, the common law, and developed a set of maxims by means of which they justified the War of the Revolution. New England was made what they considered to be a purified Old England. All men were declared to be free and equal; all were held to possess equal "natural" rights

[3] Schafer, Jos., *The Origin of the System of Land Grants for Education,* 8–10. Also Leach, A. F., *English Schools at the Time of the Reformation,* 97 *et seq.*

[4] *Report of the Commissioner of Education* (1889–1890), 1:220–23.

[5] Draper, A. S., *Origin and Development of the New York Common School System,* 31.

[6] Fiske, John, *The Beginnings of New England,* 30.

to life, liberty and the pursuit of happiness; but in the face of these high-sounding phrases, they continued the English common law with some modifications, they allowed imprisonment for debt, and they did not extend the suffrage to all males of voting age. "Intolerable restrictions burdened the life of the common man, not manhood qualifications, but tax receipts, church creeds and white skins were required of those who would vote. . . . The man without land could not be trusted. The man without piety was not to have political power."[7] To the Puritan, "freedom and liberty meant the working out of a life soberly restrained according to the will of the majority."[8] The democracy of the New England of the 17th and 18th centuries was quite different from that of Jackson, or of the present time. According to Revolutionary literature, the United States was committed to the doctrines of Rousseau; but in actual practice it more nearly adhered to the teachings of Burke.

"Calvinism is congenial to those in whom the clannish spirit is strong."[9] This clannish spirit led to the belief in the necessity of universal education and equal treatment for all men agreeing with them and adhering to their belief. The English people "had also a strong feeling of the solidarity of responsibility, which emphasized the evils inflicted on the whole people by the wrong acts of individuals and the need of national unity."[10] This feeling of a common individual responsibility for the acts of others played an important part in building up the early New England school system. The weakening of the feeling of mutual responsibility as the settlements grew and the

[7] Stevenson, R. T., *History of North America,* 12:13. Ed. by Lee.
[8] Weeden, *Economic and Social History of New England,* 1:79.
[9] Patten, S. N., *Development of English Thought,* 109.
[10] *Ibid.,* 120.

settlers became more and more independent of each other, is also a factor in explanation of the decline in educational enthusiasm at a later period. The New England colonists came over in congregations, and continued, in their new home, the old church relationships. The soil and topography of New England were not well adapted to large scale farming; consequently, the physical characteristics of the country as well as the traditions of the settlers tended to strengthen the political power of the local units. Towns, modeled after those of England, were formed, and land was held both in severalty and in common. The owner of a small holding was necessarily more or less dependent upon his neighbors,—a condition unlike that which existed under the southern plantation system. The products and services of neighbors were frequently exchanged. The idea of interdependence and of mutual influence became firmly and deeply implanted in the minds and hearts of the New England people. Severalty implanted interdependence and individuality; commonalty produced a feeling of solidarity.[11] The southern plantations were more nearly self-supporting units than the small New England farms; and commonalty was lacking in the South. "There was no mutual dependence among plantations such as would have been observed if the estates had been small, which would have signified a division of labor."[12] The latter type of life developed a class of self-reliant, liberty-loving men; it tended to exalt the importance of the individual, to produce a more exaggerated form of individualism than developed in New England.

In studying the development of education in early New England it should also be remembered that the

[11] Weeden, 1:60.

[12] Bruce, *Economic History of Virginia in the 17th Century*, 2:568.

right of taxation was carefully guarded, resting chiefly with the local units; and the close connection between religion and politics must not be overlooked. "The support of the ministers, at first voluntary, became a regular item of civic expense; they were generally chosen in open town meeting. Taxes were levied for the support of religion, and attendance on worship was compulsory. The franchise depended on connection with the church in Massachusetts and Connecticut."[13] Differences in religious belief did not at this time complicate the educational problem in New England.

In 1642, twenty-two years after the landing of the Mayflower, the first law relating to education in Massachusetts, was passed. This law asserted that the state had the right, and indeed that it was the duty of the state, to see that every child was educated. This Act gave the selectmen power to investigate as to the training of all children under their jurisdiction. If the parent was found to have neglected his duty in this important matter, he was liable to a fine. This law made education compulsory, but it made no provision for schools or for teachers. The teachers were the parents or private tutors. The head of every family was in duty bound to educate his children in order to promote the religious and moral well-being of the community in which he lived. This educational law is comparable to the modern sanitary laws of our cities which require every householder to keep his house and dooryard in a healthful and clean condition, in order that his property may not become a menace to the community and a center of infection. In both cases the police power of the state is invoked.

Thus elementary education was at this period in the handicraft or household stage of development, and was

[13] Weeden, 1:68–9.

demanded primarily on religious grounds. Education was normally a part of household industry; and it was confined to a narrow range of subjects. Public bounty was first extended in New England to the colleges, not to what we now call the common schools. Reading, writing, and arithmetic were acquired as were shoemaking or weaving. Not until the local environment was broadened into a more general one by increased population, coupled with manufacture in factories and better means of communication, did education, or could it, except of course in the case of a few specially favored individuals, expand beyond this rudimentary stage. Educational advance is very similar to the development of many industries. Indeed it might be said that there are three stages, namely, purely domestic, handicraft and factory.

After the passage of the second Massachusetts law in 1647, we find supplemented by family instruction, "the outlines of a complete system of popular education in Massachusetts,—the elementary, the grammar or secondary schools and the college—all supported by the contributions of the people, private beneficence, public taxation and legislative grants."[14] The ordinance of November 11th, 1647, reads in part as follows:—"It being one of the chief projects of that old deluder, Satan, to keep men from the knowledge of the Scriptures, as in former times by keeping them in an unknown tongue, so in these latter times by persuading by the use of tongues, that so at least the true sense and meaning of the original might be clouded by false glosses of saint-seeming deceivers, that learning may not be buried in the grave of our fathers in the church and commonwealth, the Lord assisting our endeavors:—

"*It is therefore ordered,* that every township in this

[14] *Report of Commissioner of Education* (1893–94), 1:656.

jurisdiction after the Lord hath increased them to the number of fifty householders, shall there forthwith appoint one within their town to teach all such children as shall resort to him to write and read, whose wages shall be paid either by the parent or masters of such children, or by the inhabitants in general by way of supply, as the major part of those that order the prudentials of the towns shall appoint; *Provided,* those that send their children be not oppressed by paying more than they can have them taught for in other towns; and *It is further ordered,* that where any town shall increase to the number of one hundred families or householders, they shall set up a grammar school, the master thereof being able to instruct youth so far as they may be fitted for the university: *Provided,* that if any town neglect the performance hereof above one year, that every such town shall pay five pounds to the next until they shall perform their order."[15] Three items in this act should be noted:—First, the school system is to be organized primarily in the interest of religion; second, public taxation for the support of schools is made optional with the local administrative units; third, the town, not the parent, is held responsible for the execution of the provisions of the act. In 1671 and again in 1683 the above mentioned penalty was increased, tending to show, as Hinsdale points out, a waning interest in education.

The course of events in Connecticut ran in similar channels. "The early records of the Town of Hartford are lost. The first mention of the school is in 1642, seven years after the first loghouse was erected,—when an appropriation of thirty pounds is settled upon it, not as a

[15] Reprinted in *Report of Commissioner of Education* (1892–93), 1232. See also *The Colonial Laws of Mass.* (Boston, 1889. Reprinted from edition of 1660), 190–91.

new thing, but as one of the established interests of the town—a thing to be looked after, as much as the roads and bridges, the support of public worship, and protection against the Indians."[16] In 1650 an educational law was passed modeled after the Massachusetts Act of 1647. Interference on the part of the state in educational matters was justified by "the indifference and indulgence of many parents and masters." In Rhode Island the strong opposition to the influence of the clergy was an important factor in delaying the development of the public school system. "Here the idea prevailed, as it always has in England until very recently, that the public elementary schools are charitable institutions."[17]

There was little uniformity as to educational development. Some towns were zealous in the cause; but others were extremely negligent. The constant pressure exerted upon the towns by the Colonial government aided greatly in the general development of education. The leaders who were sent to the general court were well-educated, religious men. Here is the phenomenon of a trained, selected leadership imposing educational requirements in the name of religious and civic welfare of the community.[18] It may be well to point out, at this place, that in the period, 1820–1850, the striking features of the phenomenon will be found to be considerably modified. The humanitarian leaders of the later period, however, seemed to be the true successors of the religious leaders of Colonial times. A paragraph from the writings of a local historian throws more light upon the early situation. "It was not because there was a popular demand for the school that the school came; it was be-

[16] *Barnard's Journal of Education* (1857), 4:658.
[17] Perrin, 26.
[18] Schafer, *Land Grants for Education,* 21.

cause the men who influenced public sentiment—the best men in the Colony—led the people, and would take no refusal, that at last the public feeling rose to the task of supporting the school. For though the government of the towns was democratic, and every church member had a vote, the best men nevertheless took the place and the power which their education and capacity gave them, and dragged the lagging sentiment of the populace up to the demands of the times."[19] In the elementary schools stress was laid upon the inculcation of moral virtues, and the grammar schools and colleges were intended as schools preparatory for teaching and preaching. "Finally the pious spirit of the ancient inhabitants of Woburn manifested itself in their care for the religious education of their children and youth.—Regarding religion themselves as the principal thing; they were earnestly solicitous to inculcate the same great truth on the minds and hearts of their offspring."[20]

The general education which the mass of the New England people received during the Colonial period has often been overestimated. In support of this opinion, the views of several writers will be quoted. "In those days, there was little civil law, or medicine, or book learning outside the clergy. All there was backed by the influence of property, went to regulate the towns, and to balance any excessive tendencies of the religious element."[21] "The people of Colonial New England were not all well-educated, nor were all their country schools better than old field schools. The farmer's boy, who was taught for two winter months by a man and two summer

[19] De Forest, H. P., *History of Westborough, Mass.,* 100. Also Schafer, 14.

[20] Sewall, *History of Woburn, Mass.,* 66–7.

[21] Weeden, 1:87.

months by a woman, seldom learned more in the district school than how to read, write and cipher."[22] The prominence given to the grammar school and to religious instruction and the strict supervision exercised by the ministers over the schools, makes Supt. Draper's charge against the early English schools appear pertinent also to the schools of Colonial New England. The English treated "the elementary schools with indifference," and they desired "to educate leaders to the tenets of the state church, so far as religion might go, and who would sympathize and agree with the English aristocracy, so far as politics were concerned."[23] In like manner the New England leaders were solicitous for that kind of education which tended to maintain the existing religious belief and to preserve their leadership. As late as 1821 it was written of New England that "education was entirely in the hands or under the direction of the clergy, who were all Independents and Calvinists."[24]

In the South, as we have seen, economic conditions were radically dissimilar. The difference between the early New England settlers and those of Virginia and the Carolinas was not alone sufficient to produce great variations in their attitude manifested toward education. Tobacco, cotton, rice and indigo are crops favorable to the formation of the plantation system and the use of indentured and slave labor. Fiske asserts that "the economic basis of that community [Virginia] was the cultivation of tobacco on large plantations and from that single economic circumstance resulted"[25] most of the peculiar social features of southern life. After 1646 there

[22] Fiske, *Old Virginia and her Neighbors,* 2:251.

[23] Draper, *Origin and Development of the N. Y. Common School System,* 31.

[24] Tudor, Wm., *Letters of the Eastern States,* 384.

[25] Fiske, *Old Virginia and her Neighbors,* 2:175.

was "a considerable amount of compulsory education in Virginia;" but the system of isolated plantations and the absence of any community life precluded the development of such a system of schools as was found in New England.[26] In the South, therefore, a system of tax-supported schools could not be anticipated because of the wide separation of the plantations and the lack of community feeling between the people of the different plantations, because the plantation system produced a highly self-reliant and individualistic class who would naturally oppose free tax-supported education, and, lastly, because the presence of a class of indentured servants and of slaves constituted a barrier to the development of the free-school system.

During the early Colonial period education was fostered primarily on the ground of religious necessity. The public schools were supported, as a rule, by means of land grants or other appropriations, local taxation, tuition and private beneficence. In certain localities, particularly in Massachusetts, the schools became practically free.[27] This is distinctly a period of middle-class control; clergymen dominated in the management of educational affairs. Religion and education went hand in hand. In Colonial New England, the leaders, rather than the mass of the settlers, were interested in the education of the entire people; but class differentiation was not as yet an important phenomenon.

[26] *Ibid.*, 246.
[27] Martin, *Evolution of the Mass. Public School System*, 52.

2. The Period of Transition

EDUCATIONAL DECLINE

In New England during the early Colonial Period, as we have seen, the centers of educational advance were also the strongholds of the Calvinistic theocracy. As might be expected, in Rhode Island where this theocracy was never enthroned, the early educational development was dwarfed. But with the growth of new settlements, pushing farther and ever farther into the interior, aided by the constant pressure of a new and primitive environment, a new democratic spirit, a spirit which chafed under the authority of religious and educated leadership, developed and became powerful. Not only was the supremacy of the early New England Church threatened by this rising spirit of democracy with its accompanying diversity of creeds, but the extreme and unwise zealousness of its own ministers tended to produce a reaction against it. After the crusade against witchcraft at Salem, it has been pointed out, the authority of the ministers began to wane.[1] Writers on the history of Christianity in the United States record a period of religious decline. "By the end of the first third of the eighteenth century, New England, politically, ecclesiastically, theologically, and morally, had come into a state of unstable equilibrium."[2] 1662–1720 "was a period of marked reli-

[1] Cobb, *The Rise of Religious Liberty in America*, 237.
[2] Bacon, *A History of American Christianity*, 105.

gious declension in all the colonies."[3] In 1678, Increase Mather asserted:—"The body of the rising generation is a poor, perishing, unconverted, and except the Lord pour down his Spirit, an undone generation. Many are profane, drunkards, lascivious scoffers at the power of Godliness."[4] The commercial depression of 1740, "fell upon a generation of New Englanders whose minds no longer dwelt preeminently upon religious matters, but who were, on the contrary, preeminently commercial in their interests."[5] Nevertheless, in spite of these changes in the sentiment of the people, the ministers remained, at least until the time of the downfall of the Federalist party, a powerful political factor in New England.

If, as has been maintained, early Colonial education was a growth fostered particularly by the religious leaders, an educational declension would be the logical result of the weakening of the ministerial authority. Such a phenomenon actually was observed.[6] Many other forces contributed their quota in producing this result, and in delaying a revival of educational zeal until after the War of 1812—over a century later. "This declension is commonly ascribed to the wars with the Indians and the French that wasted the blood and treasure of the colony [Massachusetts]; the political and social contentions that disturbed its peace; the uncertain relations that existed between Massachusetts and the Mother Country, and internal, economic, and social changes."[7] The foregoing analysis would, however, lay the stress directly upon the decline in religious ardor, and indirectly upon

[3] Dorchester, *Christianity in the United States,* 134.

[4] Quoted *ibid.,* 137.

[5] Greene, M. L., *The Development of Religious Liberty in Conn.,* 226.

[6] Hinsdale, *Horace Mann,* 9.

[7] *Ibid.,* 9.

those forces which contributed to this result. The intermittent warfare which the colonies were engaged in down to the end of the Revolution was certainly sufficient to prevent much attention being paid to education, which deals with the future rather than the immediate needs of a people.

In the early Colonial period all schools were town schools. As the population increased and became scattered, a new social condition developed. The population of a town was no longer concentrated around one church and one school-house. As a result of this expansion of population, a very important change took place in the management of educational affairs which modified, in no small measure, the progress of educational development. At first, in order to meet the needs of all the children of a town the "traveling school" was resorted to. "The traveling school reversed the usual practice; the school went to the children, not the children to the school; that is, the single town school was kept a certain time in one corner of the town, then in another, and so on until the circuit had been completed, the periods that it spent in different localities being equal or unequal, as circumstances might determine."[8] This soon led to the formation of several district schools within a given town. But as might be expected with a people accustomed to the town meeting form of government and extremely jealous of centralized control, the district system of school management followed. This process was a gradual one; the culmination of the power of the school district was not reached until 1827.[9] This year "marks the

[8] Hinsdale, *Horace Mann,* 11.

[9] Martin, *The Evolution of the Mass. School System,* 92. In Connecticut, the formation of "school societies" may have been a factor in the development of the district system.

utmost limit to the subdivision of American sovereignty —the high water-mark of modern democracy, and the low water-mark of the Massachusetts school system."[10] At this time only two limitations were placed upon the powers of the district, namely, the raising and apportionment of taxes, and the qualification of teachers.[11]

The Grammar school had been, as we have seen, the distinctive and important grade of school in the early period. The growth of the district system necessarily meant the decline of this grade of school, because the districts, being small units, could not support, in the majority of cases, a good grammar school. At this point in our history the famous academy is ushered in. This is simply the visible token of the decline in the "free" grammar school; it grows out of the demand of the well-to-do classes for better educational facilities than could be obtained in the district school. While the district system led toward democracy and equality of privilege from the political point of view on the one hand; it tended on the other toward class differentiation. This latter tendency, coupled with the growth of an industrial class, led finally to the educational awakening which placed our educational system upon a new basis, and to an era which demanded centralized school administration and tax-supported free elementary schools.

During the long period of "marking time" in educational affairs, which preceded the era under investigation, while many dissimilar forces were aiding in the disintegration of the early Massachusetts and Connecticut school system, one influence stands out prominently in opposition to the prevailing tendency, namely, the system of land grants for educational purposes. The pres-

[10] Martin, 92.
[11] *Ibid.*, 93.

ence of large quantities of land at the disposal of the towns, the colonial, and later the state, governments enabled them to subsidize the schools along the well-known line of least resistance. They could aid in the development of education without apparently touching the pocketbook of the tax-payer. "In the light of English practice respecting school support, it is not surprising to find the early American colonists founding 'free schools' or 'free grammar schools,' and endowing them with lands. The custom was followed to some extent in all of the colonies, but in certain ones, namely Massachusetts, Connecticut and New Hampshire, it developed steadily in the direction of the public land grant system. In many, perhaps in most cases, these lands, when granted, were of little value. But their value steadily increased with the general development of the country, and with this increase the popular interest in them kept pace."[12] It is worthy of notice that the system of land grants for educational purposes originated in order to aid the grammar, not the elementary or common school.[13]

The chief disintegrating forces of this long period of transition may, therefore, be summarized as follows, although it must be remembered that these are not distinct, isolated, or unrelated influences: (a) The decline in the power of the Puritan theocracy and the increasing strength of various religious sects; (b) the enlargement of the sphere of settlement, and the consequent development of the district system; (c) wars, internal dissentions and the formation of a new government distracted the attention from the field of education; (d) the decrease of mutual interdependence among the settlers and the

[12] Schafer, *The Origin of the System of Land Grants in Education*, 11, 15.

[13] *Ibid.*, 23.

weakening of the spirit of clannishness. On the other hand, the forces which tended to continue our educational progress appear to be; (a) an inherited belief in the religious and civic value of education; (b) the use of land grants for educational purposes.

Soon after the War of 1812, other forces appear in the foreground which give a new impulse to educational progress. Just at the dawn of this period, one of the earliest spokesmen of educational radicalism declared:—"Under our present constitution, or for the last forty years, the schools have no doubt been vastly improved. But they have most certainly, not kept up with the progress of society in other respects. Although their absolute motion must be acknowledged, their relative motion has been for many years retrograde. And there never was a time, since the settlement of the country, when the common schools were farther in the rear of the improvements of the age in almost everything else affecting our condition and happiness than they are at the present moment."[14]

THE SITUATION AT THE OPENING OF THE PERIOD (1820–1850)

What then were the educational conditions in the different states at the opening of the period under consideration? The Constitution of Massachusetts in 1780 stated that it was the duty of "legislatures and magistrates," to cherish the interests of literature and the sciences, and all seminaries of them: especially the university at Cam-

[14] Carter, J. G., *The Schools of Mass. in 1820* in *Old South Leaflet,* No. 135, 3.

bridge, public schools, and "grammar schools in the town." The school law of 1789 was still in force in 1820. This law is conceded to be a step backward in comparison with previous laws.[15] By this act the district system was legalized. The towns were still required to maintain schools, but the minimum length of the school year was only six months. Towns of one hundred and fifty families or more were required to support a grammar school. Penalties were provided in case of neglect, by a town, to support schools. For example, a town of fifty families was fined fifty pounds for such neglect.[16] One important clause of this Act reads thus:—"*Be it enacted by the authority aforesaid,* That all plantations which shall be taxed to the support of the government, and all parishes and precincts, are hereby authorized and empowered, at their annual meeting in March or April to vote and raise such sums of money upon the polls and ratable estates of their respective inhabitants for the support and maintenance of a schoolmaster to teach their children and youth to read, write, and cipher as they shall judge expedient, to be assessed in due proportion and to be collected in like manner with the public taxes."[17] After speaking of the educational laws of this state, Winterbotham remarks:—"These laws respecting schools are not so well regarded in many parts of the state, as the wise purposes which they were intended to answer, and the happiness of the people require."[18] At the opening of our period there were no public schools where chil-

[15] Dexter, *History of Education in the United States,* 80.

[16] *Barnard's Journal of Education* (1857), 4:657–710.

[17] Full text of the law given in *Report of Commissioner of Education* (1892–3), 1234–37. Also, *The Perpetual Laws of Mass.* (1801), 2:39–44.

[18] *An Historical, Geographical and Philosophical View of the U. S.* (1795), 2:177.

dren could prepare for the grammar schools. In 1817, a sub-committee of the School Committee of Boston was appointed to consider the desirability of public primary schools. The sub-committee reported that "for children under the age of seven years, it is true, no schools are maintained at public expense." But it was asserted, this class of children was not neglected; they were cared for in a series of small private schools. Although the tuition acted as a tax upon the parents, it was not considered to be burdensome or inequitable. The sub-committee also emphasized the importance of home training for very young children. In view of the heavy taxation already levied for public schools, it was urged that the establishment of free primary schools for children under seven years of age was not "expedient."[19] At the opening of the period of educational revival, in Massachusetts, the state whose educational history is proudly pointed to by students of history, elementary education, although legally a part of the duty of the public schools, actually devolved, in the main, upon private schools.

Until 1798, Connecticut towns were required to maintain schools, supported, in a three-fold manner, by a state fund, local taxation and tuition. According to the provision of laws enacted in 1795 and 1798, the control of the schools passed into the hands of local "school societies." Local taxation was made optional. As a consequence the schools, as a rule, only remained open long enough to expend the money granted out of the general fund, but no longer.[20] New Hampshire, in 1719, enacted

[19] Report signed by Chas. Bullfinch, Chairman, was printed in full in the *National Intelligencer,* November 29, 1817, 1. Also, see Wightman, *Annals of the Primary Schools of Boston;* and Hinsdale, *Horace Mann,* 32.

[20] *Barnard's, Journal of Education* (1857), 4:657–710.

the Massachusetts school law of 1647; and, in 1721, provided that a fine be imposed upon the selectmen personally, if they neglected to maintain a grammar school as provided by law.[21] Nevertheless, this was not well enforced.[22] In 1748, for example, the town of Chester voted "that the town defend and secure the selectmen from any damage they may come to for not providing a Grammar school."[23] Governor Wentworth in his message in 1771 declared that "nine-tenths of your towns are wholly without teachers or having vagrant teachers . . . worse than none . . . unknown in principle and deplorably illiterate."[24]

Among the New England States, Rhode Island has an educational history which is peculiarly her own.[25] She did not enact a common school law until the year 1800; and this was not enforced, but instead was repealed three years later. In 1796, Samuel Slater "established at Pawtucket a Sunday school at which was taught the rudiments of knowledge. His efforts were supplemented by those of John Howland at Providence, who as a barber was a member of the Association of Mechanics and Manufacturers, a society organized in 1789. By the energy of Howland the General Assembly in 1800 was led to pass an act creating free schools."[26] "Not until 1828 was such

[21] Robinson, M. H., *History of Taxation in New Hampshire* in *American Economic Association Publications,* 3d series (1902), 3:178. Primary authority, *Laws of N. H.* (1726), 133, 160.

[22] *Ibid.,* 178.

[23] Chase, *History of Chester,* 278. Quoted by Robinson. See also Secomb, *History of Amherst,* 319.

[24] Quoted by Robinson, 179, from *N. H. Provincial papers,* 7:287.

[25] The unique agricultural features of Rhode Island are well described in a monograph: Channing, Edw., *The Narragansett Planters* in *Johns Hopkins Univ. Studies,* 4. The methods employed in agriculture in Rhode Island closely resembled those of the plantation system in the South.

[26] Richman, I. B., *Rhode Island,* 279.

a law put upon the statute books that remained there,"[27] and this law was practically a dead letter, outside of Providence, until after the extension of the suffrage in the decade of the forties. "The literature of this state [Rhode Island in 1795] is confined principally to the towns of Newport and Providence. . . . The bulk of the inhabitants, in other parts of the State, are involved in greater ignorance, perhaps, than in most other parts of New England."[28]

In the state of New York, "the first state legislation regarding schools seems to have been made in 1786, when it was ordered that unappropriated lands within the state should be laid out in townships ten miles square, and that in each of them one section should be reserved for the 'gospel and schools' and one 'for promoting literature.' Special appropriations were also made to help academies."[29] Nine years later, a general law was passed appropriating one hundred thousand dollars annually for five years. This money was paid directly out of the State Treasury. The law was not reenacted, however, at the expiration of the five years. As late as 1806 there were none save parochial and private schools in the city of New York, and the public school society was then formed to care for the education of a large number of children already outside the educational charge of the various religious sects.[30] This was a private society composed of influential citizens. It controlled the public schools of the city of New York for nearly half a century. The significant fact is that this society was originally formed to supplement the work of religious organizations.

[27] Hinsdale, *Horace Mann*, 25.
[28] Winterbotham, 2:237.
[29] Dexter, *History of Education in the United States*, 77.
[30] *Report of Commissioner of Education* (1893–94), 698.

The Constitution (1790) of Pennsylvania contained the following section:—"The legislature shall as soon as conveniently may be, provide for the establishment of schools throughout the state in such manner that the poor may be taught gratis. The arts and sciences shall be promoted, in one or more seminaries of learning." In 1802 this section was carried into effect by enacting a law entitled, "An act to provide the education of the poor gratis." This law, strengthened in 1804 and 1809 remained in force for over thirty years. But the attempt to provide free schooling for the poor was not successful. "Out of the failure to educate the poor as a class arose the idea of schools free to all."[31] Much of the work of education in this state devolved upon religious societies, and other private schools; the poor children were often sent to these schools at public expense. "Almost every religious society have one or more schools under their immediate direction, for the education of their own youth of both sexes, as well of the rich, who are able to pay, as of the poor, who are taught and provided with books and stationery gratis."[32] The following newspaper account of a Shaker school is interesting in this connection. "The Shakers are now regularly organized into a school district by themselves under the sanction of the law. . . . We hazard nothing in the assertion, that there is not in the county, not perhaps in the state, a school, where children from the age of four to nine, would compare to those of the Shakers, in readiness of reading prose, rhyme, or blank verse, or in accuracy of spelling, punctuation and emphasis."[33]

[31] Jenkins, *Pennsylvania, Colonial and Federal,* 3:31.
[32] *Winterbotham* (1795), 2:423.
[33] *Pittsfield Sun,* May 10, 1822. Copied in *Baltimore Morning Chronicle,* May 25, 1822.

In New Jersey, Delaware and Maryland at the opening of the period of educational revival, conditions as to education were similar to those already portrayed in Pennsylvania. In 1820, New Jersey passed an act authorizing townships to raise money for the education of the poor. Delaware, in 1817, appropriated one thousand dollars for each county for the instruction of poor children; but these "pauper schools" did not prosper.[34] In Maryland many benevolent societies were organized to provide instruction for the indigent. The following is an extract from the Annual Report of the Male Free School of Baltimore. "It is truly gratifying to the trustees to witness the increasing interest, taken in the education of the poor,—to see the talents, the zeal and the means now employed to give instruction to the indigent youth." "To the liberality of the citizens of Baltimore, they [poor boys] are indebted for the ample means of instruction which they now enjoy, . . ."[35]

The famous ordinance of 1787 consecrated the Northwest to freedom, and proclaimed that "religion, morality, and knowledge, being essential to good government, schools, and the means of education, should forever be encouraged." The first Constitution of Ohio, the first state to be carved out of the Northwest Territory, contained the following clause:—"schools and the means of instruction should be forever encouraged by legislative provision, not inconsistent with the right of conscience." The first general school law was not passed until 1821, nearly a score of years later; and this was unsuccessful. Previous to this law, education in Ohio was purely a private matter. Many schools were organized by means of private subscription; many private houses were uti-

[34] Dexter, 59.
[35] *Baltimore Morning Chronicle,* December 10, 1822.

lized as schoolhouses.[36] "Schools worthy of remembrance, between 1802 and 1820 were known only in most enterprising towns."[37] The slow development of public education is made evident by the following quotation. "In the year 1833, there were twenty-four private schools in the city [Cincinnati], with thirty-eight teachers and one thousand two hundred and thirty pupils, and in the public schools but twenty-one teachers and two thousand pupils."[38] At the beginning of our period, Ohio, Indiana, Illinois, Michigan, and Wisconsin, were still frontier states. Education was necessarily much neglected; but the influential settlers, as a rule, adhered to the early New England view as to the necessity and value of universal education. In the South, excepting South Carolina, prior to 1820 there was practically no provision made in any state for public education.

In New England, excepting Rhode Island, at the beginning of our period, the principle of free tax-supported schools for all was, in theory, accepted. Elsewhere free public elementary education was only for the poor. But even in New England the free schools were much less efficient than private ones. Rev. Edward Everett Hale in *A New England Boyhood* said that there was no thought of sending him to a public school, —too poor in character.[39] The difference between New England and other sections was in reality only one of degree. However, this difference changed slightly the character of the struggle during the period of educational revival. In New England, the demand was nominally for supervision; but supervision signified better free tax-sup-

[36] *Life and Times of Ephraim Cutler,* 49, 88, 172.
[37] *Barnard's Journal of Education* (1859), 6:82.
[38] Venable, *Literary Culture in the Ohio Valley,* 421.
[39] Hinsdale, *Horace Mann,* 30, foot note.

ported schools, it stood for a leveling of the invidious distinctions between public and private schools. In New York and Pennsylvania, particularly in the latter, on the other hand, the issue was clear-cut; it was definitely and unmistakably "free" versus "pauper" schools.

3. Fundamental Influences

The foregoing chapters have given us a view of the conditions at and preceding the opening of this important period in our educational and industrial history. We have before us the traditional and inherited beliefs and tendencies in regard to education. The attention must now be directed to the changes, social and industrial, which occurred during the period. This epoch (1820–1850) is one of rapid transformation from household industry to the factory system; it is the era of the extension of the suffrage, of the abolition of imprisonment for debt, of various humanitarian movements from religious revivals to the establishment of communistic settlements, from temperance reform to the abolition of slavery. During this period the growth of the cities was rapid, an important labor movement arose, and the theory of protection received recognition from Congress. Brief consideration will now be given to various changes, industrial, social and political which appreciably influenced the development of the public school system.

THE GROWTH OF POPULATION AND OF MANUFACTURE

The year 1790 may be selected as the date of the birth of the factory system in this country. The first factory within the borders of the United States was erected in

Beverly, Massachusetts, in 1787. This venture was unsuccessful.[1] From this time until the end of the period under consideration, there was a gradual transfer of industry from the household or the small workshop to the factory. With the development of the factory system came the concentration of industry in the towns, more minute division of labor, and rapid increase in the production of manufactured articles. The percentage of population living in towns and working in manufacture and trades increased at a rapid rate. The Embargo Act and the War of 1812 caused capital to shift from commerce to manufacture, particularly in New England. During this period, importation was greatly reduced; and this fact tended, in a measure, to stimulate invention and home manufacture. "At all events, we know that the embargo and the war did cause the introduction of numerous manufactures on a larger scale than ever before; and that those who engaged in the business had a natural monopoly."[2] But while the manufacturing interests were benefited, the shipping interests were seriously injured; and shipping regulations adopted by other nations subsequent to the war further increased their distress. The business of ship-building came to a standstill; and many ships lay idle in port.[3]

Immediately after the War of 1812, and the close of the European struggle with Napoleon, this county [*sic*] was flooded with foreign manufactured goods. The infant industries, for such they might then justly be termed, having been artifically [*sic*] stimulated by the restrictions laid, in the immediately preceding years, by the embargo

[1] *The Factory System of the U. S.* in *Census Reports,* 1880, *Manufactures,* 2:6–7.

[2] Stanwood, *American Tariff Controversies,* 1:128.

[3] Stanwood, 1:164; and *Niles' Register,* 11:374.

act and the conditions of war, were unable to meet the excessive competition; and an era of hard times set in, which continued until after 1820.

The entire period (1820–1850) is characterized by the rapid growth of urban population, the development of manufacture, and a multiplicity of important inventions. The population of Massachusetts increased during the two decades, 1800–1820, nearly 24 per cent.; during 1820–1840, over 40 per cent.; during 1830–1850, nearly 60 per cent.; but during the same periods the increase in the population of the city of Boston was approximately 73, 115, and 123 per cent. respectively.[4] Lowell, which had no existence in 1820, boasted of a population of over 20,000 in 1840; New Bedford increased from 3,947 to 12,-087 during the same space of time. "Lowell is a mere manufacturing village, and no place, we believe, has ever increased from manufactures alone, with greater rapidity, or with the same population, has had an equal number of operatives. In 1830, its population was 6,500 and in December 1833, it was estimated at 15,000; and more than one-third of these were employed in cotton establishments."[5] In 1790 less than one-twentieth part of the total population of Massachusetts lived within the limits of city of Boston; in 1820, about one-twelfth part, and in 1840, about one-eighth part were inhabitants of that city. "Within ten miles of Boston there is now (1846) one quarter part of the population of the state, amounting to more than 200,000, chiefly dependent upon Boston as the center of business; in 1790 the number was less than a ninth part of the whole."[6] Chickering shows that 213

[4] In 1830, the population of Boston was 61,392; Providence, 16,833; New York City, 202,589; Philadelphia (city and county), 161,427; Pittsburg and Allegheny, 18,000; Cincinnati, 24,831.

[5] Pitkin, Thos., *A Statistical View of the Commerce of the U. S.*, (1835), 523.

[6] Chickering, *On Population and Immigration*, 109.

towns chiefly agricultural, situated in Massachusetts, increased only 8.5 per cent. from 1820 to 1840, while 88 manufacturing towns increased 79.62 per cent.[7] During the score of years from 1820 to 1840, the population of Rhode Island increased approximately 31 per cent., that of the city of Providence nearly 100 per cent.; in New York State the increase was nearly 77 per cent., while in the city of New York the percentage was about 153 per cent.; in Pennsylvania the increase was over 64 per cent., and that of Philadelphia over 72 per cent.[8]

In the three New England States of Massachusetts, Rhode Island and Connecticut during the period from 1820–1840, the number of persons engaged in agriculture increased approximately one-fourth; those engaged in commerce decreased about one-third; and those engaged in manufacture and trades increased nearly two and one-half times.[9] Owing to inaccuracies and to different classifications in the two census reports these figures can only be considered approximate; but they show clearly the drift toward manufacture. In 1840, according to the census reports in Massachusetts, the number of persons engaged in agriculture was 87,837, in commerce, 8,063, in manufacture and trades, 85,176; in New York, 455,954, 28,468, and 173,193 respectively; in Ohio, 207,533, 15,-338 and 105,883 respectively. The number of cotton factories in the United States increased from 801 in 1831, to 1,240 in 1840. In 1831, the number of persons employed in cotton manufacture in Massachusetts was 13,343, and in 1850, 28,730; in Rhode Island, 8,500 and 10,875 respectively.[10]

The immigration into the United States during the

[7] *Ibid.*, 49.

[8] *Census Reports;* also Tucker, *Progress of the U. S.*

[9] *Ibid.*, Tucker, 135–36.

[10] *The Factory System of the U. S.* in *Census Reports,* 1880, *Manufactures,* 8 *et seq.*

decade, 1820–1830, was 143,439; during the next decade, 599,125, and during the period 1840–1850, it increased to 1,713,251. From 1830 to 1837 the immigration increased nearly three and one-half times.[11] A census of the city of Boston taken in 1845 stated that 37,289, or 32.6 per cent. of a total population of 114,366 consisted of foreigners and their children. The state Census of New York (1845) found that more than one-eighth of the whole population were of foreign birth, and more than one-third of the inhabitants of New York City were foreign born.[12] The character of the population was rapidly changing. Many foreign immigrants were finding homes in the North Atlantic States, and many of the home stock were migrating westward.

Among the important inventions and innovations of this period of thirty years are many which practically revolutionized industrial methods, for example, the general introduction of the power loom, the use of the hot-air blast in iron smelting, the introduction of anthracite coal into the same industry, the inventions of the mower, the reaper, the sewing machine and the friction match, the introduction of the steam printing press, the use of the screw propeller on steam boats, and the invention of the steam hammer for steel working. Methods of transportation and communication changed even more completely than did those employed in manufacture. The Erie Canal was completed in 1825. The succeeding ten or fifteen years saw a rapid development of canal systems in the Northern States. The use of steamboats which began before the opening of this period, increased at a

[11] *Immigration into the U. S. from 1820 to 1903,* (U. S. Treasury Dep't.), 4336, 4339.

[12] Chickering, *On Population and Immigration,* 35. Article on foreign immigration.

rapid pace. But more important was the development of the railroad system. The first steam railroad, three miles in length, was built in 1826. In 1840 the mileage of the steam railroads of the United States was 2,640 miles; in 1850, 9,021 miles. Locomotive construction in the United States began about 1830. The first telegraph line was constructed in 1844.

THE EXTENSION OF THE SUFFRAGE

The extension of the privilege of casting the ballot, which was an interesting and important phenomenon of the first half of the nineteenth century, is closely connected with the educational movements of the times. Both are parts of the democratic movement which aimed at benefiting the masses; the extension of the suffrage enabled the workers congregated in the cities, to become important factors in the political arena, thus giving their demands a potency which otherwise would have been lacking. Four influences seem to be chiefly responsible for the new suffrage enactments:—The belief in the revolutionary dogmas of natural right and of the equality of men, which had been strengthened by the impulse received from the French Revolution; the intense democratic spirit fostered by the frontier; the strength of the newly formed working classes living in the rapidly growing towns and cities; and the competition of political parties for voters.[13]

Aristocracy, royalty and inequality were feared because of past experience. Washington, Adams and Hamilton were opposed because of their alleged aristocratic tendencies. Jefferson represented, to a degree, a reaction.

[13] Blackmar, F. W., *The Chautauquan,* 22:31.

Jackson, however, was the first representative of the frontier. He broke the long line of New York and Virginia men who represented an aristocracy of birth and training. Jackson stood for the reaction against trained leadership. This democratic movement which culminated in the election of Jackson had been gathering strength for years; it united the farmer of the West and the working population in the cities.

"The frontier states that came into the Union in the first quarter of a century of its existence came in with democratic suffrage provisions, and had reactive effects of the highest importance upon the older states whose people were being attracted there. An extension of the suffrage became essential. It was western New York that forced an extension of the suffrage in the constitutional convention of that state in 1821; and it was western Virginia that compelled the tide-water region to put a more liberal suffrage provision in the constitution framed in 1830, and to give the frontier region a more nearly proportional representation with the tide-water aristocracy."[14] "Of all the states west of the mountains, she [Tennessee] was the only one that adopted in all their vigor the old restrictions on the subject." [Property and religious qualifications for voting and office holding.][15] But with the growth of the cities and towns, and the formation of a considerable wage-earning population, we find, in the towns and cities, an important element demanding an extension of the suffrage. In Rhode Island, in 1824, a vote was taken on the question of the adoption of a constitution. Providence was the stronghold of those favoring the adoption. "After 1825 the agitation was

[14] Turner, F. J., *American Historical Assoc. Reports,* (1893), 222.
[15] McMaster, J. B., *Acquisition of Political, Social and Industrial Rights,* 48.

wholly in the hands of the suffragists;" and after 1829 it became very important.[16] The proposed constitution of the "legal" convention of 1842 in Rhode Island was rejected chiefly by the vote of Providence. The following is the summary of the vote:[17]

	For	Against
Providence county	2,570	5,343
Newport county	1,459	516
Kent county	784	838
Bristol county	683	238
Washington county	1,181	813
Total	6,677	7,748

The *New York Journal of Commerce* stated "that the constitution thus rejected is a different thing from that which is called the free suffrage constitution which was the result of a popular movement, and sustained by most of those who opposed the constitution thus rejected."[18] In Rhode Island the cities and the working classes fathered the suffrage movement which in other states was forced by the frontier.

Professor Blackmar makes the following statement regarding the removal of the religious tests relating to the exercise of the suffrage. "From this time on, [1691] the freehold test became more general until at the beginning of the eighteenth century it was nearly universal in practice in the colonies. The religious test became less exacting in many instances, and finally broke down altogether on account of the great diversity of religious beliefs of the new immigrants, rendering it impossible to maintain a

16 Mowry, *The Dorr War,* 35; also McMaster, *ibid.*
17 *Niles' Register,* April 2, 1842, 62:80.
18 Quoted, *ibid.,* 62:85.

popular government under a religious test."[19] This argument, if tenable, ought also to account for the removal of the property qualifications in the first half of the nineteenth century. During this period class differentiation increased, and the opposition between rural and urban districts began to be clearly discernable. Social antagonism shifted from the religious to the economic point of view.

The West—the frontier—did much to force more liberal suffrage provisions; and the ballot in the hands of the wage-earners was an important factor in making tax-supported schools an actuality. The latter statement is supported by these facts which will be considered later: (a) Workingmen's conventions and parties during this period, favored tax-supported schools; (b) the cities rather than the rural districts supported the movement. The following testimony from English experience is pertinent. "If factory regulation had been attempted, though only in a piece-meal way, sometime before we had been a democratic house of commons, the same can not be said of educational law. It was the parliament elected by a more popular suffrage in 1868 that passed, as we know, the first great educational act. That act introduced compulsory schooling."[20] Frederick Jackson—a representative labor leader,—voiced a similar sentiment from the view point of the workingmen when he declared in January, 1867:—"Nothing will force the governing classes to recognize the workingmen's claim and judge them fairly, until they find them wresting into their own hands real political power."[21]

[19] *Chautauquan,* 22:29.
[20] Green, T. H., *Works,* 3:339.
[21] Quoted by J. B. Andrews, in *The Commons,* June, 1905, 346.

THE HUMANITARIAN MOVEMENT*

Two movements now attract our attention: the humanitarian and the labor movement of the period under consideration. It is not for us in this study to consider these important social movements in detail; but they are so inextricably connected and interwoven with the educational advance of the period that we must note the sources of these two movements, and notice the causes which led to their decline or dilution. After the termination of the War of 1812 came a period of anxiety and distress for the artificially stimulated manufacturing industries which the War and the Embargo Act had fostered. This period terminated in the crisis of 1819. With the revival of industries, beginning about 1822 and becoming quite apparent in 1825, came the rapid growth of town population, the stimulation of immigration; and a new set of industrial and social problems were placed before the people of this young republic, particularly those residing in the northern and eastern states. The peculiar evils of modern urban life became apparent; but experience gained from rural life afforded no adequate guide as to the proper and effective methods of coping with these new evils. Idle and uneducated children appeared upon the streets of the cities and towns, on the one hand; and on the other, the problem of child and woman labor in factories or in intensive domestic industry, pressed for solution. The rush into the towns, the consequent change from outdoor and active, to indoor and comparatively sedentary life, and the greater opportunity for association with others, made more noticeable, if it did not actually increase, the evils of intemperance. Pauperism

* See article by the writer in *The International Journal of Ethics*, October, 1906.

and crime became crying evils. Societies for the prevention of crime, for the aid of the poor, and for other benevolent purposes, sprang as by magic into existence.

As early as 1813, a "Society for the Suppression of Intemperance" was formed in Massachusetts. The "Pennsylvania Society for the Promotion of Public Economy" was founded in 1817; and a similar society was organized in the same year in New York City. Juvenile crime became especially noticeable in 1820 and 1821. The American Temperance Society was organized in 1826.[22] Public meetings were called to consider measures to better social conditions. "From such earnest efforts to prevent pauperism and crime there sprang most naturally a discussion and revision of the means then employed to reform criminals and lessen the repetition of crime, in short, of criminal codes and penitentiary systems in use in the States."[23] The prevalence of juvenile crime turned attention toward the matter of education. The long continued hard times accentuated the evils of the factory town and the industrial city, and produced a fertile soil out of which sprang public interest in the reformation of morals, and the humanitarian movement.[24]

Several quotations, taken chiefly from contemporary writers may make the picture clearer. In 1819, it was calculated that the number of persons in Pittsburg thrown out of work by the depression from 1816–1819, was 1,288; in Philadelphia, in thirty branches, 7,288. In Rhode Island alone, in the cotton industry, the number employed was diminished, 1816–1819, by 11,337.[25] In 1826, Rev. Joseph Tuckerman resigned his pastorate in Bos-

[22] McMaster, 4: ch. 37; also *Hist. of N. America,* 12: 436, Ed. by Lee.

[23] McMaster, 4:540.

[24] *Ibid.,* 4: ch. 37.

[25] *Franklin Gazette,* February 12, 1821.

ton, and devoted himself to the interests of the poor. "He found the streets filled with idle children, large families occupying the damp and dirty cellars of Broad and Sea streets, graduating thence to the hospitals and alms-houses. Indefatigably visiting from house to house, giving practical counsel, apprenticing boys, procuring employment for adults, starting an infant school, attending the courts, the whole problem of poverty, ignorance and vice now absorbed him, heart and head."[26] In 1833, it was reported that 6,069 criminals and vagrants were committed to local prisons in New York City; and the number of public paupers was estimated to be 24,326,—making a total of 30,395, or about one-eighth of the total population of that city. The amount of public money needed for the support of these classes of the population was about $300,000. The number of dramshops in the city of New York in the year 1833, was approximately 3,000.[27]

The following statistics, representing the total for the states of Virginia, Maryland, Delaware, Pennsylvania, New Jersey, New York and the New England states, give an idea of the amount of woman and child labor in the cotton industry during the opening years of the decade 1830–1840: Males employed, 23,301; females, 39,178; children (under 12 years of age), 5,121.[28] In the cotton mills of the Union Manufacturing Company of Maryland, in 1822, there were employed 120 girls, 58 boys (7–19 years of age), and 6 men.[29] Mr. Carey published a pamphlet in which he stated "that there are in the four Northern cities, probably from 18,000 to 20,000 women who, if constantly employed for sixteen hours out of the

26 Tiffany, *Chas. Francis Barnard, His Life and Work,* 14.

27 Quoted from *N. Y. Observer,* by *Amer. Daily Advertiser,* February 11, 1835.

28 *Easton, (Md.) Republican Star,* April 3, 1832.

29 *Ibid.,* December 10, 1822.

twenty-four, cannot, on an average, earn more than $1.25 per week."[30] A correspondent to *Niles' Register* in 1816, makes a cold blooded calculation as to the additional amount of wealth which might accrue to the United States, if children, not now employed, could be placed in the mills and factories of this country. Such a step, it was argued, would benefit commerce and agriculture as well as manufacture.[31]

This interesting phenomenon, known as humanitarianism, was a product of the social and economic change and unrest of the period.[32] Certain educated leaders and literary men are found advocating better conditions for workingmen, and presenting high ideals to the American people. The prominent humanitarian and educational leaders of the period, such as Emerson, Thoreau, James G. Carter, Geo. Ripley, J. F. Clarke, Wm. E. Channing, Horace Mann, Henry Barnard, Robert Rantoul, Jr., O. E Brownson, Theodore Parker, Samuel Lewis and F. H. Hedge, came chiefly from old New England stock; they were sons of ministers, farmers and merchants, and they were nearly all college bred.[33] But they were only remotely connected with the great industrial changes which had been sweeping over New England. These men

[30] *Niles' Register,* 38:141.

[31] *Ibid.,* 11:86.

[32] Humanitarianism, as it manifested itself in the United States at this time, is by no means an isolated and unique phenomenon. It seems to arise in every complex society in a period of acute social antagonism when the lower classes are struggling for better conditions. Prof. Dunning observes that it is a "familiar phenomenon" to find radical views based upon reactionary institutions. (*Political Theories from Luther to Montesquieu,* 77–78). The French Revolution and the fall of Japanese feudalism present to the student of history two very striking climaxes of humanitarian movements. In these two instances the controlling classes seem to have become enthused with the spirit of self-sacrifice mixed with fear.

[33] See Appendix II, for short biographical sketches of these men.

were representatives of a class in the community which was losing its grip upon social and political authority. As one writer states, "a feeling was abroad that all things must be new in the new world."[34] This feeling was in reality produced because the ground was being cut out from under the very class which had hitherto molded the ideals and directed learning of New England. Another student of this period looking at this phenomenon from an entirely different point of view makes the following statement: "The commercial classes of New England robbed of their functions as a ruling class, while still retaining a sufficient wealth to maintain them were dying out in a blaze of intellectual fireworks."[35] This produced the transcendental movement,—a branch of the more inclusive humanitarian movement.

Let us, however, examine a little closer into this humanitarian movement which plays such an important role in the educational progress of the period. Why should its leaders turn toward measures for the improvement of the workingmen? As Nieboer has pointed out, in slave countries a slave is personal property, and the slave is held by the master or employer by means of personal compulsion. On the other hand, in countries where modern industrial system has developed and laborers are plentiful, the workers are obliged to seek employment through impersonal compulsion. At one end of the chain is the slave economy where the owner has a direct personal interest in the slave or worker; at the other end is the modern factory owner with no direct personal interest in his hired workmen.[36] Between these two extremes stand serfdom and the domestic system of industry

[34] Frothingham, *Transcendentalism in New England,* 106.
[35] Simons, A. M., *Class Struggles in America,* 22.
[36] Nieboer, *Slavery as an Industrial System,* 419 *et seq.*

with its peculiar and intimate relations between apprentices, journeymen and masters. New England witnessed, at the beginning of our period, a rapid destruction of the crude and unsystematic forms of the domestic system of industry, and the adoption of the factory system, or of a more intensive and systematic form of domestic industry. Contemporaneous with this evolution came necessarily and inevitably a considerable modification in the relations existing between employers and employees. The new class of employers was not connected to employees by any customary or intimate relations. Now, the class of men from which came the humanitarian leaders was, as has been noted, intimately connected with the other classes of the community. These men were still strongly influenced by the ideals and customs as to the treatment and care of workers, which prevailed under the old form of the domestic system. The influence of custom here as elsewhere in the economic world was such as to soften the rigor of the competitive system.[37] At this particular time, custom stood for better treatment of the working classes; it urged the necessity of a paternalistic attitude on the part of the employers toward employees. The humanitarian leaders were not directly influenced by the economic motives which so rapidly changed the point of view of the manufacturing interests; and it must not be forgotten that the roots of this movement were nourished in the soil of eighteenth century idealism.[38]

The humanitarian leaders wished to continue the old semi-paternalistic method of domestic economy into modern industrial and city life. They saw the existing

[37] Webb, *Industrial Democracy,* 2:695 *et seq.*

[38] "The individual's conscience is apt to be the mirror of the particular environment in which he has grown up; and even his revolt against existing institutions bears traces of its unavoidable influence." Ritchie, *Natural Rights,* 85.

evils of child and woman labor, pauperism, juvenile crime, intemperance and unemployment; they were strongly impressed by the disintegrating effects, upon the family, of crowded city and town life; and they magnified and glorified the desirable features of the earlier form of domestic industry with its intimate personal relations between workers and employers. The hurry and bustle of business and the keenness of the race for profits offended and shocked them; and no golden stream was finding its way into their pockets to obscure their vision of conditions, past and present. The humanitarian leaders saw a new class of men rising to control not merely the wealth, but the political and social affairs, of the state and nation. They were animated by very different ideals and motives from those which appealed to this new economic and social class. The two classes were instinctively antagonistic; and the humanitarians struggled against that which seemed to them to be evil. These men more or less unconsciously joined hands with the new-born labor movement. These two dissimilar forces united in aiding in the educational advance toward tax-supported schools. Educational progress was most marked in the cities where these two forces developed their greatest strength.[39]

THE LABOR MOVEMENT

In this study, it is not wise to enter into an intensive consideration of the labor movement which waxed and waned during the period which we are examining. Its in-

[39] Recently in England a similar phenomenon may be noticed. "The Socialist leaders and the most notable spiritual descendants of Cobden and Mill" were united on the question of free trade and the South African war. Hobhouse, *Democracy and Reaction.*

ception was, of course, the natural, or rather the inevitable, result of the aggregation of workers in towns and factories. "Organized labor is labor in its normal condition."[40] Four phases of this movement may be distinguished: (1) The development of trade unions; (2) co-operative or communistic activity; (3) the birth of workingmen's parties and the participation of workingmen in the political activities of the time; (4) the appearance of journals and newspapers devoted to the cause of labor.[41] This labor movement was ephemeral and in one sense premature; conditions were not yet ripe for permanency. The peculiar importance of this evanescent movement was due, not to the solidity and strength of its internal organization, but to external conditions, to the peculiar balancing of divergent interests which obtained at this particular period in the history of the United States. "Five industrial classes were at this time struggling for the mastery in America. The plantation South in alliance with the pioneer West held the reins of power. However, their interests were by no means identical and there were many points of disagreement concerning a political program. In the North the commercial class was just giving way to the manufacturing class and arrayed against this latter were the new social forces of the proletariat."[42]

Even if this bald mathematical statement of the resolution of the social and political forces of this era, is not correct, it certainly is true that at this time there was great diversity of interests. It is perhaps sufficient to point to the election of John Q. Adams as President, and to the

[40] Ely, R. T., *The Labor Movement in America*, 34.

[41] *Ibid.*, chs. 2 and 3; also, Simons, *International Socialist Review*, 5:146–7.

[42] Simons, A. M., *Class Struggles in America*, 21.

bitter struggle and changing attitude as to the tariff, to illustrate the point that here was an excellent political opportunity for the rapidly increasing working population. It was this unique situation which gave the workingmen a peculiarly strategic political position. It has been pointed out that the argument that protection would tend to raise the rate of wages was not injected into tariff discussions until after the rise of a laboring class.[43] In the city and state of New York and in Philadelphia, after the Workingmen's Party had exhibited considerable strength the old parties hastened to conciliate the workers and to dissipate their political strength by adopting important planks of their platform, or by placing some of the candidates or friends of the workingmen upon their tickets.[44] The success of Martin Van Buren, Jackson's chief lieutenant in the important State of New York, was, in no small measure, due to keeping in close touch with the labor vote.[45]

Although this movement soon lost its strength, it left an indelible impress upon our institutions. Many forward steps were taken which have not, as yet, been retraced. The reasons for its disintegration may be briefly summarized under five headings. (1) A strong permanent labor organization is not to be anticipated while much practically free land can be obtained; and while it is possible for the employee to pass easily and readily to the position of employer. Under such conditions class consciousness and the feeling of solidarity of interests among the workers do not readily develop to a sufficient

[43] Mangold, G. B., before economic seminary, Univ. of Wis., 1905.

[44] *New York Spectator,* October 30, 1830; *Working Man's Advocate,* March 13, 1830. Myers, G., *History of Tammany Hall,* 97 *et seq.; Mechanics' Free Press,* (Phila.) September 20 and 27, October 18, 1828.

[45] Simonds, J. C., *The Story of Labor in All Ages,* 438.

degree to insure strong and permanent labor union organizations. (2) The attainment of many of the more moderate demands of the labor party and labor press, such as a mechanic's lien law, abolition of imprisonment for debt, and increased taxation for the public schools, naturally reduced the number of adherents and diminished the ardor of those remaining. (3) Coupled with this was the rising tide of the slavery agitation which drew the attention from the demands of the workers and absorbed much of the vigor of the humanitarian leaders. (4) The stigma of infidelity which became attached to the workingmen's party was a serious handicap. A New York newspaper in discussing the success of the "Infidel" or "Fanny Wright" ticket (which elected a state assemblyman in 1829), after having enumerated its chief demands, said: "Principles like these, we are persuaded, would be regarded with utter abhorrence by the great body of 'mechanics' and 'workingmen' who were so artfully enlisted in their support."[46] Yet there was nothing in the published platform which savored of infidelity or of anarchy. (5) The communistic movement was also an important factor in weakening and dissipating the strength of the workingmen's organization. This movement also absorbed a portion of the strength of the humanitarian movement. The Workingmen's Party in New York City was first split on the question of agrarianism. A few months later the most important branch of the party was divided into two sections on the subject of education. The weaker wing stood for the boarding, or communistic, school; and the other for improvement in the familiar common school system.[47]

[46] *New York Mercury,* November 11, 1829.

[47] The writer, *The Workingmen's Party of New York City, 1829–31* in *The Political Science Quarterly,* Sept., 1907.

4. Arguments for and against Education

The problem which now confronts us, baldly stated, is What were the forces engaged in the struggle for free tax-supported public schools? The antecedent balance of forces, and the important industrial and social changes of the period of struggle have been considered. The question directly before us presents itself under two closely connected aspects. First: What were the arguments advanced during this period for and against free tax-supported schools, and to what classes or interests in the community did each argument particularly appeal? Second: What was the actual alignment of the various interests,—social, industrial and religious?

The arguments for the free tax-supported schools, or for educational advance, may be summarized under seven heads. These are arranged approximately in the order of importance: (1) Education is necessary for the preservation of free institutions. (2) It prevents class differentiation. (3) Education tends to diminish crime. (4) It reduces the amount of poverty and distress. (5) It increases production. (6) Education is the natural right of all individuals. (7) Education will rectify false ideas as to unjust distribution of wealth. It will be noticed that arguments 1, 2, 6, and 7 relate to civic and ethical considerations; and 3, 4 and 5 to economic considerations. The arguments against the above proposition may be arranged as follows: (1) Free education for all increases taxation unduly. (2) Taxation for the purpose of maintaining free public schools is a violation of the rights of the individual. (3) A public system of schools was opposed by certain religious elements because of possible injury to particular religious sects. (4) Certain non-English speaking people opposed the public schools because they feared that their own tongue would be supplanted by the English language. (5) Impractical legislation caused much opposition. (6) It was urged that education would not benefit the masses. (7) Injury to the private school was alleged. (8) Public education tends to break down social barriers. In addition, as influences acting adversely to educational progress may be mentioned the increasing opportunity to put children to work in factories, and a wide-spread apathy and indifference toward education which was evident in certain sections and among certain classes in the community. It is more difficult to classify these opposing forces; but 2, 3, 4 and 8 may be labeled as purely conservative forces, and 1 and 7 as of economic nature.

The idea that universal education is essential to free institutions is inherited from Colonial New England. This was the favorite argument of the man from New England. We find it used for example by Thaddeus Stevens and Samuel Breck in Pennsylvania, and by Samuel Lewis and Ephraim Cutler in Ohio. In general, this argument was advanced by two quite different elements in the nation,—the well-educated leaders influenced by early New England ideals, and the laboring classes. Its advocates approached the question from two viewpoints. On one hand, it was urged that free institutions, could not long exist or could not progress without wide diffusion of education. "A self-governing people without education is an impossibility; but a self-governing people, imperfectly and badly educated may continually thwart itself, may often fail in its best purpose, and often carry out the worst. More especially will this be the case, if the power of wealth, and the power of knowledge failing to co-operate because one or the other is placed in a false position, act in destructive contradiction to each other."[1] The above quotation from an address delivered, in 1839, by Robert Rantoul is perhaps a typical statement of the argument. Governor Clinton of New York, at the opening of the Session of the State Legislature in 1827, said: "The great bulwark of republican government is the cultivation of education; for the right of the suffrage cannot be exercised in a salutary manner without intelligence."[2] "In a republican government, general intelligence should be diffused among its citizens. They are thus enabled to perform their duties as constituent parts of the government."[3] Governor Seward of New York in his message (1839) declared: "The consequences of the most partial improvement in our system of education will be wider and more enduring than the effects of any change of public policy, the benefits of any new principle of jurisprudence, or the results of any enterprise we can accomplish."[4]

The following two quotations present the same view from the standpoint of the workingmen. The first shows clearly a feeling of class antagonism. "Indeed, to conceive of a popular government devoid of a system of popular education, is as difficult as to conceive of a civilized society destitute of a system of industry. This truth has been generally received in this country, and never, I believe, directly denied; although its force has been at-

[1] Rantoul, Robert, Jr., *Memoirs,* 134.
[2] Randall, *History of the School System of New York,* 27.
[3] Gov. Porter, in inaugural address, 1839, (Pa.) *Connecticut Common School Journal* (1839), 1:80.
[4] *Ibid.*

tempted to be evaded by the rich, who have heretofore, unfortunately, been our sole law makers, through the odious system of charity schools—the bare idea of which impresses a consciousness of degradation, and leads to results the very reverse of those that ought to be produced by popular instruction."[5] This spirit of discontent is one phase of the movement which found concrete expression in the election of Andrew Jackson. A paper devoted to the interests of farmers and laboring classes voices the sentiment in the following trite statement. "But few out of the many can receive more than a common school education.—Give to every child this and our Republic is safe."[6]

The second viewpoint emphasized the social side of the question, and argued that universal education was necessary to promote the common welfare. Accordingly, education was held to be a public affair; the essence of this view is the same as that which animated the men of Massachusetts when they placed the Act of 1642 upon the statute books. "It is vain to say that education is a private matter, and that it is the duty of every parent to provide for the instruction of his own children." Some parents will not, others can not. "The State has an interest in every child within her limits."[7] Thus argued Bishop Doane to the people of New Jersey in 1838. A legislative committee in the same state declared that the duty of education is a constitutional one. "In the first place the power over education is one of the powers of the public police, belonging essentially to government. It is the duty of self-preservation, according to its actual

[5] Simpson, Stephen, *A Manual for Workingmen,* (1831), 201.

[6] *Farmer's and Mechanics' Journal,* (Alexander, N. Y.) April 7, 1838.

[7] *Report of Commissioner of Education,* (1867–68), 314.

mode of existence, for the sake of the common good."[8] The Secretary of the Commonwealth (Pennsylvania) in a communication to the House of Representatives of that state, used this argument: "If the maxim is true, that knowledge is power, and liberty itself but a precarious blessing without it, then its general diffusion becomes the common interest of all our citizens, in proportion to the extent each may have, personal and pecuniary, to defend and protect."[9] Seth Luther in his address on the "Education of Workingmen," delivered in 1832, expresses the radical position of the workingmen. "In our review we have seen a large body of human beings ruined by a neglect of education, rendered miserable in the extreme, and incapable of self-government; and this by the grinding of the rich on the faces of the poor, through the operations of cotton and other machinery."[10] Luther emphasizes the evils of the factory system, dwelling particularly upon the evils of long hours and child labor. He holds that the factory system with its overwork, unhealthy conditions and accompanying crowded home conditions is rendering the "common people unfit to govern themselves," because the physical energies of the operative, "man, woman or child, are wasted and his mind is rendered supine."[11] In 1850, the supporters of the School Law of New York, passed in 1849, stood firmly on the ground that a tax to support schools was justified on the ground of social utility. "We hold, therefore, that our present school tax is not imposed on the rich for the benefit of the poor; but imposed on the whole State for the benefit of the State."[12] The constitutionality of this

[8] *Ibid.*, 323, 324.
[9] *Philadelphia Liberator*, June 29, 1833.
[10] Pamphlet, *Education of Workingmen*.
[11] *Ibid.*
[12] *New York Tribune*, September 28, 1850.

law was attacked because the legislature authorized a referendum to the people in regard to this law. It was claimed that the legislature had no right to delegate its authority by making the enactment of this bill rest upon the verdict of the people as expressed at the ballot box.

Universal education will prevent class differentiation, and will tend to give all children equal opportunities in the battle of life. This argument, of which three different phases may be distinguished, is a natural outgrowth or survival of the spirit which animated the American and French Revolutions. While it was originally urged by the middle class, it was later seized upon and loudly proclaimed by the rapidly increasing class of wage-earners. The spokesman of the workingmen at this time played continually upon this string, as the following quotations indicate. This fact may be considered as an indication that the growth of cities, the increase of division of labor, and the gradually widening separation of employer from employee, had progressed far enough by the beginning or the middle of the decade, 1830–1840, to produce a marked class differentiation and a sharp differentiation of interests.

Simpson in his afore-mentioned book, which was dedicated to the shade of Jefferson, declares that, "it is to education, therefore, that we must mainly look for redress of that perverted system of society, which dooms the producer to ignorance, to toil, and to penury, to moral degradation, physical want and social barbarism."[13] The same writer complains of the arrogance and pride of the educated; and adds, the "educated are generally rich." "Literature and education, thus affianced to opulence, naturally feel a strong repugnance to share their intel-

[13] *A Manual for Workingmen,* 214–15.

lectual dominion with the mass of society."[14] The retention of the "common law of Great Britain" was, he held, a vital error, as it is incompatible with equality in government. "A State of Society exists in this country which prevents the producing classes from a participation in the fountains of knowledge, and the benefits equally designed for all." This condition is produced and sustained by "Avarice, which is nurtured and fostered by a defective education."[15] The *Delaware Free Press* declared its mission to be "to awaken the attention of Working People to the importance of cooperation in order to attain the rank and station in society to which they are justly entitled by virtue of their industry, but from which they are excluded by want of a system of Equal Republican Education."[16] In 1835, a *Miners' Journal* urged that the school law of Pennsylvania would tend toward equality for individuals and toward the permanence of republican institutions. "The Education Law is emphatically the Poor Man's Friend."[17] One of the toasts given at a Workingmen's banquet, on July 4, 1830, read as follows: "Universal Education.—The nation's bulwark; a fortress that will alike defy the siege of aristocracy, and the ravages of time."[18]

Horace Mann adhered emphatically to this view. "Education, then, beyond all other devices of human origin, is," he said, "the great equalizer of the conditions of men,—the balance-wheel of the social machinery."[19] As

[14] *Ibid.*, 24–5.

[15] Luther, Seth, Address previously cited.

[16] *Delaware Free Press,* January 9, 16, and 23, 1830. Also, *Free Enquirer,* (N. Y.) November 21, 1829, 29.

[17] Quoted in *American Daily Advertiser,* (Phila.), January 21, 1835.

[18] *Free Enquirer,* July 17, 1830, 304.

[19] *Education and Prosperity,* in *Old South Leaflet,* No. 144, also *12th Report.*

early as 1795, Samuel Adams pointed out the dangers of the private academy. He feared that it would detract from the value of the common school, and lead to class distinctions between rich and poor.[20] The evils which these men were combating were real, not imaginary. We learn that in Massachusetts, "in 1838–39 there was spent for instruction in private schools—not incorporated—one-half as much money as was spent for the common schools,—wherever the private-school system in any community gets on its side the social and political leaders, it will grind the public schools to the wall, and do it under legal and constitutional sanction."[21] An investigation into the common school systems of New England and New York by an official committee from a western state furnishes contemporary evidence on this point. "Indeed, they [Schools of New England and New York] are already, in some cases, particularly in Connecticut, producing that very discrimination between rich and poor, which above all things they aim to prevent and are accelerating the classification of the members of society according to their wealth. Only allow the rich (no matter under what pretext, whether of philanthropy, or patriotism, or interest) to prescribe the education of the poor, and they prescribe their conditions and relative importance."[22] The leaders of the movement in New England for school supervision saw clearly that if the public school was to be beneficial to the masses, it must be approximately as efficient as the private school.

The two following quotations throw light upon the western and southern view as to the efficacy of education as a leveler of invidious class distinctions. A legislative

[20] Martin, *Evolution of the Mass. Public School System,* 128.
[21] *Ibid.,* 129–30.
[22] *Barnard's Journal of Education,* 5:136–37.

committee on common schools, in Ohio, reported (1825), the system of free schools "seems most consonant to the principle of our constitution. It places the children of the rich and poor more nearly upon a level and counteracts that inequality which birth and fortune would otherwise produce."[23] Even in the South during this period are found advocates of a system of public schools. About 1830, the *Southern Free Press,* published in Charleston, South Carolina, stated in its prospectus, "Our great object will be to urge you to break down the barrier which separates your children from those of lordly aristocrats by the establishment of national schools."[24]

The economist must recognize the importance and correctness of the plea that education does tend to equalize opportunity, although today our definition of education would be broader than that of the men of 1830–1840. Wages of individuals vary greatly from the wage received by the common day laborer to the salary received by the skilled professional man; and the difference between the two rates of compensation is by no means solely due to differences in the expense of training workers for the two dissimilar positions in life, or to absolute differences in efficiency, but in a large measure to a monopoly or "forced" gain, or rent of ability accruing to the specialist. "In fact, every enlargement of education, in so far as it makes for greater equality of economic opportunity, tends to reduce differential rents of employment and likewise the marginal specific rents which are seen to depend upon them."[25] While education tends to reduce rents of ability of all kinds, it does not, of

[23] *American Journal of Education,* (1827), 2:437.
[24] *Free Enquirer,* December 26, 1829, 71.
[25] Hobson, J. A., *Economics of Distribution,* 339.

course, attack, directly at least, other forms of "forced" or monopoly gains.

The men who have, up to this point, presented the argument that education prevents class differentiation, have evidently had in mind a system of public day schools. But one branch of the workingmen's party in New York, of which Robert Dale Owen was a member, declared in favor of more radical educational methods. This position is well illustrated by extracts from a committee report prepared in May, 1830. "Your Committee propose, therefore, a System of Public Education, which shall provide for all children, at all times, receiving them at the earliest age their parents choose to intrust them to the national care; feeding, clothing, and educating them to the age of maturity. Your Committee propose that all the children so adopted should receive the same food; should be dressed in the same simple clothing; should experience the same kind of treatment; should be taught (until their professional education commences) the same branches; in a word that nothing savoring of inequality, nothing reminding them of the pride of riches, or the contempt of poverty, should be suffered to enter these republican safeguards of a young nation of equals. . . . The food and clothing might be chiefly raised and manufactured by the pupils themselves, in the exercise of their several occupations. . . . Your Committee do not propose that anyone should be compelled to send a child to these public schools, if he or she saw fit to have them educated elsewhere. But we propose that the tax should be payed by all parents, whether they send their children or not."[26] Education of

[26] *Working Man's Advocate,* (N. Y.), June 19, 1830. This report was undoubtedly inspired by the writings of the two Owens and Miss Frances Wright. See, for example, an address of Frances Wright,

the boarding school type became the most insistent demand of this branch of the Workingmen's Party. It was stoutly maintained that the question of day versus boarding schools was vital. Upon this point there could be little opportunity for compromise. General education "is the chief—we had almost said the only—essential in our political creed. We admit that the common school system of New England is calculated to do good—that it has done good. But it cannot regenerate a nation; the proof is that it has not. . . . Let those who desire common day schools speak out at once. They do not desire the regeneration of this country."[27]

The Agrarian wing of the party was, however, still more radical. It was asserted that all educational measures, although highly desirable, were rendered, "in a measure, abortive" by the existing inequality in social and economic conditions. "Political dreamers! Reformers, if ye prefer that I shall call you so! Feed first the hungry; clothe first the naked, or ill-clad; provide comfortable homes for all; by hewing down colossal estates among us, and equalizing all property; take care that the animal wants be supplied first; that even the apprehension of want be banished; and then you will have a good field and good subjects for education. Then will instruction be conveyed without obstacle; for the wants, the unsatisfied wants of the body will not interfere with it."[28]

The three arguments supported chiefly upon economic

---

delivered in Philadelphia and printed in the *Free Enquirer,* December 12, 1829, 51; a series of articles taken from the *New York Daily Sentinel,* published in the *Free Enquirer,* May 1 to 15, 1830; and *An Outline of a Rational System of Education,* in *The Crisis,* May 26, 1832.

[27] Quoted in the *Working Man's Advocate,* May 29, 1830, from the *New York Sentinel.*

[28] Skidmore, Thomas, *Rights of Man to Property,* (1829), 369.

grounds, may be conveniently classed together. It was declared that universal education diminished crime, prevented poverty, and increased production. The frequent use of these arguments seems to be due largely to the phenomenon of hard times; and its distressing effects upon the industrial population of the cities. It was felt that something was wrong; and it was believed that philanthrophy [*sic*], temperance reform and a protective tariff could not alone cure the evils which afflicted the working people. The peculiar conditions during this period of unusual industrial development caused the formation of this almost fanatical and wide-spread belief that education of the narrow type then prevalent, would markedly reduce the amount of poverty and crime in the land, and would cause the worker to become a more efficient producer. Although these arguments greatly exaggerated the influence which a purely intellectual education can have upon the prevalence of crime or of poverty, or upon the efficiency of a workman, they were important factors in the struggle for tax-supported schools, and they appealed to a class in the community who were in a large measure indifferent as to all the other arguments advanced.

Horace Mann was one of the chief exponents of the importance of education from the economic point of view. He declared in his Report for 1846 that if education was merely demanded as a basis for good citizenship in a republican form of government, a monarch would be justified in opposing it. Therefore, Mann sought more universal and fundamental foundations upon which to build the system of public schools. "Beyond the power of diffusing old wealth it [education] has the prerogative of creating new." For the creation of wealth, "intelligence is the grand condition."[29] "That po-

[29] Mann, Horace, *Report of 1848* in *Life and Works of Horace Mann,* 4:252, 259.

litical economy, therefore, which busies itself about capital and labor, supply and demand, interest and rents, favorable and unfavorable balances of trade, but leaves out of account the element of a wide-spread mental development, is naught but stupendous folly."[30] He also asserts that education is a preventive of crime and vice. "The property of this commonwealth [Massachusetts] is pledged for the education of all its youth up to such a point as will save them from poverty and vice, and prepare them for the adequate performance of their social and civil duties."[31] Mann's firm belief in the efficacy of education as a cure for the social and economic ills of society led him to enunciate a doctrine which has a distinctly modern ring. "The successive holders of this property are trustees bound to the faithful execution of their trust by the most sacred obligations; and embezzlement and pillage from children and descendants have not less of criminality, and have more of meanness than the same offences when perpetrated against contemporaries."[32]

An early American economist and college president states the case in an interesting and convincing manner; and, if we read a broad meaning into the terms, "intellectual" and "knowledge" his argument might be accepted at the present time. "Intellectual cultivation tends to increase the industry of a people in two ways: First, by exciting a people to exertion; and, Second, by directing that exertion . . . Ignorant people are indolent, because they know neither the results that may be accomplished, nor the benefits that may be secured by industry. . . . But, it is evident, that improvement in knowledge, in order to

[30] *Ibid.*, 260.

[31] Mann, Horace, *Report of 1846* in *Life and Works of Horace Mann*, 4:131.

[32] *Ibid.*, 132.

be in any signal degree beneficial, must be universal. A single individual can derive but little advantage from his knowledge and industry if he be surrounded by a community both ignorant and indolent. In just so far as other men improve their conditions, and become useful to themselves, they become useful to him; and both parties thus become useful to each other. This is especially the case where a government is, in its character, popular; that is, where laws emanate from the more numerous classes. In such a case, not only is an intelligent person not benefited, but he is positively injured, by the ignorance and indolence of his neighbors."[33] An ardent supporter of the Maryland optional school law passed in 1826 attempted to convince the rich that the law was beneficial to them. "Although the poor will doubtless derive incalculable benefits, the rich will receive the greater gain, inasmuch as their greater riches will thence obtain its greatest protection and security . . . from the best assurance of good government, to-wit, the general diffusion of useful knowledge amongst the great body of the people."[34] Again he urges that "as in proportion to the amount of property is the protection of that interest to be estimated, so, in the like manner are they [the wealthy] concerned in the general intelligence of the common people."[35]

Rantoul told the workingmen that "the main object of government is the protection of persons and property, and this object will be more effectually secured by the general education of the people, than by any penal code, however rigidly enforced."[36] Simpson informs us that

[33] Wayland, Francis, *Political Economy,* (copyright 1837), ch. III, sec. 5.

[34] Teackle, L. D., *Easton (Md.), Republican Star,* July 4, 1826.

[35] *Ibid.,* July 11, 1826.

[36] Rantoul, Robert, Jr., *Speech to Workingmen of America* (1833) in *Memoirs,* 240.

"knowledge is the grand remedy of intemperance." Out of the West came this literary gem:—"Far better to pay taxes which will rise like vapors to descend in refreshing showers, than to build jails, penitentiaries and almshouses, to relieve wretchedness and punish crime which a wholesome education might have prevented."[37] Channing was a most earnest and able advocate of education for the working people. In his essay, entitled, "The Elevation of the Laboring Classes," is found this significant statement. "The impulses which are to reform and quicken society, are probably to come, not from its most conspicuous, but from its obscurer, divisions; and among these, I see with joy new wants, principles and aspirations, beginning to unfold themselves." The most radical and optimistic view of the economic significance of education naturally is held by the communists of this period. The creed of Robert Dale Owen illustrates the extreme position taken by this class of reformers. "I believe in a National System of Equal, Republican, Protective, Practical Education, the sole regenerator of a profligate age, and the only redeemer of our suffering country from the equal curses of chilling poverty and corrupting riches, of gnawing want and destroying debauchery, of blind ignorance and of unprincipled intrigue."[38]

The opinion that education is a natural right of all individuals is quite closely related to the first argument in this list. Daniel Webster evidently had both ideas clearly in mind in an address which he delivered in 1822. New England, he said, "early adopted and has constantly maintained the principle that it is the undoubted right, and the bounden duty of government, to provide for the instruction of all youth. For the purpose of public instruction, we hold every man subject to taxation in pro-

[37] Lewis, Samuel, *Report of 1845* in *Ohio School Journal,* 1.
[38] *Free Enquirer,* November 7, 1829, 14.

portion to his property, and we look not to the question, whether he himself have, or have not, children to be benefited by the education for which he pays. We regard it as a wise and liberal system of police, by which property, and life, and the peace of society are secured."[39] Mann in his Tenth Report declared that every human being has an absolute right to an education; and held that the education of the laboring class "enables the workingman to eat the fruits of his labor." We may dismiss this argument by noting that it is the logical outgrowth of the theory that man is endowed with certain inalienable rights.

The last plea for the affirmative is a somewhat unique one, fathered by a writer on political economy. "Education universally extended throughout the community, will tend moreover to disabuse the working class of people in respect of a notion that has crept into the minds of our mechanics, and is gradually prevailing, that manual labor is, at present, very inadequately rewarded, owing to combinations of the rich against the poor; that mere mental labor is comparatively worthless; that property or wealth, ought not to be accumulated or transmitted; that to take interest on money lent or profit on capital employed is unjust. These are notions that tend strongly toward an equal division of property, and the right of the poor to plunder the rich. The mistaken and ignorant people who entertain these fallacies as truths, will learn, when they have the opportunity of learning, that the institution of political society originated in the protection of property."[40] This writer is surely a forerunner of the managers of recent "campaigns of education," for various partisan or special reasons. In opposition to the gen-

[39] See *Report of Commissioner of Education,* (1867–68), 327.

[40] Cooper, Thomas, *Elements of Political Economy,* (1829), 333–4.

erally accepted view, this advocate of universal instruction asserted apparently that education is a conservative force,—an influence which stiffens existing law and custom instead of tending to level social and economic differences. But would the adherents of these two apparently conflicting views agree upon a definition of the term "education"?

As might reasonably be anticipated the most vital arguments against the public school system center around the necessary increase in the amount of public taxation which must result from any enlargement or considerable improvement in the system. The great stumbling block in the path of educational progress during this era was taxation. The land grant system, however, as has been noted, reduced, in a measure, the difficulties arising from this obstacle. The economic arguments in favor of free schools were concerned chiefly with the improved efficiency of those who would become workers in a few years hence, or with the prevention of pauperism and crime a decade later. In prosperous times when the numbers of unemployed and pauper classes were somewhat reduced, these arguments did not appeal directly and concretely to the tax-payer; in fact at no period could they be expected to forcibly appeal to persons living in rural districts. On the other hand, stands opposed the immediate, tangible results of an increase in the tax-rate. Education deals with the future; taxation bears down today. It was simply a case of increasing present individual expenses with a view to future general good, to the public welfare some years hereafter. Herein lay the great strength of the argument that all improvements in the public school system would increase direct, visible taxation, and increase it inequitably.

Other arguments in favor of better public educational

facilities centered around civic, ethical and sentimental motives. Where these come directly into conflict with present, although perhaps short-sighted and insufficient, economic motives, unless a high ideal is raised and accompanied by patriotic zeal or religious ardor, they are almost sure to fall by the way-side. It was easy for the taxpayer to justify non-support of a public school system, exactly as it was not difficult for the southern plantation owner to present plausible arguments in favor of a continuance of the institution of slavery. Both phenomena spring originally from the same fountain head,—the temporary economic interests of the individual, or of a group of individuals. Just as the northern man lacked this economic interest in regard to slavery, so the workingmen and the smaller taxpayer, did not feel the force of the argument based upon increased taxation. They considered this view to be sordid and selfish; their pocketbooks were not visibly depleted, and their children attended the free public schools.

The following quotation concerning the struggle for public tax-supported schools in Pennsylvania, in 1834 and 1835, illustrates how bitter was the opposition which arose through the increase in taxation. "There were taxes, and there is no more certain method of stirring up public opinion of a virtuous thrifty and frugal people, such as then inhabited Pennsylvania, than by pricking their pocketbooks. They were willing to have reform, provided it did not come high, or they were not compelled to pay for it. A violent reaction arose. Nearly half the districts in the State rejected the act or contemptuously ignored it."[41] From New England comes similar testimony. "However the dominant Calvinistic theology of Puritan Massachusetts may have theorized

[41] McCall, *Life of Thaddeus Stevens*, 35.

concerning 'fixed fate' and 'foreknowledge absolute,' practically it recognized in every village community a free moral agent, acting out its own volitions and drawing upon itself the consequences of its own freedom. Out of this grew the individuality so characteristic of Massachusetts towns: some open to new influences, looking always toward the east, ready to welcome the rising sun, generous in sentiment and provision, always in the van of social progress; others narrow, petty, parsimonious, burning incense to the past rather than offering sacrifices to the future; not because they reverence the past so much; but because incense is cheaper than oxen or sheep, or libations of wine and oil."[42] In another section the same author declares that the Massachusetts law of 1826, which established high schools in every town of the state, was opposed by two elements; the academies and private schools, and by the inhabitants of the agricultural towns.[43] This would tend to place the rural towns in the incense-burning class.

In New York during the agitation of 1849 and 1850, the matter of taxation played the chief role. The *New York Tribune* stated "that the backbone of the opposition [to free schools] is hostility to be taxed to school other men's children—that is to the free school principle in any form."[44] A correspondent to the *Plaindealer* published in Roslyn, Queens County, declared that he considered the "present [1849] odious School Law" as "worse than highway robbery." Clark Rice, a wealthy citizen of Watertown, New York, in a letter defined a free school law in emphatic terms. "What is a Free School Law? Allow me to answer, it is in one particular, a Poor-

[42] Martin, *Evolution of the Massachusetts School System,* 86–7.
[43] *Ibid.,* 197–98.
[44] October 17, 1850.

Law. It differs a little from our ordinary Poor-Law. The latter is for filling the belly and covering the back at the expense of the Tax-Payer. The former for conferring an accomplishment,—a useful one to be sure—the driving of knowledge into the head."[45] A newspaper correspondent summed up the chief arguments in the New York agitation, against the School Law, as follows:—(1) The state has no right to tax one man to pay for the education of another's children; (2) the children of the poor will grow up idle and lazy if education is provided free of charge; (3) the law was held to be the entering wedge of agrarianism and Fourierism.[46] At a mass meeting called for the purpose of opposing the School Law, and held in Jefferson, New York, "a resolution to the effect that they were strongly opposed to all taxation to support schools and to vote for no man who upheld the system, was proposed but being regarded as inexpedient, was withdrawn."[47]

In Ohio, in 1829, the passage of a law was secured which gave the city of Cincinnati the right to organize city schools, and the authority to levy special taxes to support the same. Nevertheless, "the cautious city council were reluctant to tax the people for the support of free schools the richest objecting most to what they called 'charity schools.' "[48] A curious survival of old arguments is found in a recent statement of a lecturer before a New York Study Club. "The better class of people in New York cannot afford large families. They have too much to pay in taxes to support the large families of the thoughtless poor . . . New York property owners pay in-

[45] *New York Tribune,* September 26, 1850.

[46] *New York Evening Post,* August 27, 1850.

[47] *Ibid.,* October 11, 1850.

[48] Venable, *Literary Culture in the Ohio Valley,* 421. See also Foote, J. P., *Schools of Cincinnati,* 34–7.

creasingly large taxes every year, due mainly to the enormous immigration. Who, may I ask, would want to pay taxes to educate children that should never have been brought into the world? Why should the thrifty pay for the shiftless? I am not so un-christian as to say that the child once here should not be cared for. But so long as tax-payers pay for expensive play grounds, etc., the children of the poor will increase like rabbits in a burrow."[49] Dr. Wayland appears to have held similar views. He believed that educational expenses might be provided "partly, by a general fund. This fund should, however, never defray more than a portion of the expense; for no man values highly, what he gets for nothing."[50]

The plea that free public education is a violation to the rights of the individual and an infringement upon his liberty, joins hands on the one side with the argument just discussed, and on the other side with religious opposition to a public school system. It is extremely interesting and important to notice that many of the points advanced by the men who presented this line of argument, have reappeared in more recent years, under a slightly different garb in opposition to other radical or progressive measures advocated by workingmen. The negative definition of liberty was used by those who employed this argument as a weapon directed against the public school system. Liberty was assumed to be non-interference with the individual; protection and tax-supported schools looked to government interference. The definitions of "rights" and of "individual liberty" are extremely liable to be given a class or sectarian interpretation, or to be used merely as catch phrases to snare the unwary.

[49] *Chicago Record-Herald,* November 16, 1905.
[50] *Political Economy,* 130.

Rhode Island affords an example of the extreme position taken by the opponents to tax-supported schools. "The original Providence compact to obey the government of the majority 'only in things civil' had been perverted so that education by the state was supposed to violate the religious liberty of the parent, a curious illustration of the way in which the narrowest sectarianism may fraternize with the most radical assertion of civil and religious liberty; . . . So violent was this prejudice that respectable members of the legislature declared that the attempt to tax a community for public schools 'would be resisted at the point of the bayonet.' "[51] Here is an excellent example of liberalism uniting with reactionary religious sectarianism against the more modern ideal of democracy. The force which in the earlier history of Rhode Island stood for progress, was now a conservative and retrograde influence. In 1828, a law was passed making the support of the public school optional with the towns. In 1844, 16 years later, only three towns imposed a tax for school purposes. In 1847, on the contrary, only three towns refused to impose local taxes for that purpose. This apparently sudden reversal of public opinion in this manufacturing state has been attributed to the campaign of enlightenment carried on by Henry Barnard.[52] The really significant fact is that in the early forties the long struggle for a constitution and broader suffrage qualifications ended. Immediately after this extension of the right to cast the ballot, tax-supported schools begin to increase rapidly, and by 1850 the principle was apparently established in this state, beyond controversy. If the two facts are closely related to each other; one further comment ought to be made. In 1840, according to the

[51] Mayo, *Report of Commissioner of Education,* (1896–97), 787.
[52] *Ibid.,* 784 *et seq.*

census reports, fifty-one and a fraction per cent. of all persons engaged in gainful occupations, in Rhode Island, were engaged in manufacture; or in other words a very high percentage of her citizens were wage-earners. We must not lose sight of these facts when more detailed consideration is given to influence of the wage-earning population upon the development of the public school system.

In Massachusetts, in 1839, a new administration came into power. It was suggested that the care and control of the schools should be left to "the nurseries of pure democracy,"—the town and district meeting. It was asserted that the Board of Education which was trying to introduce supervision into the schools, and to increase the power of the central authorities and weaken that of the local districts, was trying to "Prussianize" the schools. Further the new administration held that the Board was attempting to substitute aristocratic for democratic measures,—an ingenious device for crushing the liberties of the citizens of the commonwealth. This view did not prevail in the legislature, and the Board of Education was allowed to continue its work.[53] A writer discussing opposition to free education, has stated the arguments as follows;—"But these opponents of free education object to any compulsory proceedings on the part of the State, alleging that a law of this character, if passed, would be a violation of the liberty of the citizen, who has a right to do as he pleases, to educate his children or not, as he pleases, to worship God or not, as he pleases, and to live free from any restraint of any kind, whether civil or moral."[54] It would not be difficult to find arguments advanced in opposition to labor unions, collective bargain-

[53] Martin, *Evolution of Massachusetts School System,* 178–79.
[54] Duffield, D. B., *Barnard's Journal of Education,* 1857, 3:95.

ing, or an eight-hour day, which rest upon the same foundations and repeat almost identical phrases.

A strong defender of the cause of public schools and a friend of the working classes, makes a rather long statement of the situation, but one which seems worthy of quotation. "A system of general education, one would hardly imagine, could meet with an opponent in an age so enlightened and so philanthropic—an age so distinguished for the march of mind, the diffusion of knowledge, and a severe scrutiny into all the principles that combine in the structure of society. And yet, wonderful to say, public education for the people has gothic adversaries, and illiberal, narrow-minded traducers. The extension of the lights of knowledge by popular education, to all the people of the republic, has ever been the avowed object of our most illustrious statesmen. The text of the friends of liberty was—to enlighten the people is to promote and cement the public virtue. The soundness of the text was never questioned anterior to the organization of a party, whose object it was to obtain it from the legislature as a right, unjustly withheld. When public instruction was bestowed as a boon of charity, it found numerous advocates, and met with no opponents; but now when we justly demand it as a right—and under our constitution it must be a right and not a charity—it is not only refused by some, but to our utter amazement, its consequences are painted as baneful to the people, and deprecated as having a fatal tendency upon the good order of government. We seem to have resuscitated from the tomb of time the very spirit of the feudal ages, in the breasts of certain bigots, intolerants, aristocrats, and narrow-minded monopolists of knowledge, who seem as averse to giving the people light, as they are to paying them for their labor in hard money."[55] Several

[55] Simpson, *A Manual for Workingmen,* (1831), 212–13.

states which authorized in their constitutions, or by-laws, the formation of a public school system, allowed these laws or constitutional provisions to be dead letters for years. When an attempt was finally made to enforce the laws or carry out the requirements laid down by the constitution, violent opposition immediately arose. It appears that there are grounds for the contention made in the latter part of the quotation. One other feature of interest in the above quotation is the use of the term "liberty." It is quite evident that Simpson has abandoned the narrow negative definition, it means something positive to him.

To conclude the discussion of this argument, it may be well to present a clause quoted from resolutions purporting to have been drawn up at a New York State mass meeting in 1850. These resolutions give us an inkling into the bitterness of the fight on tax-supported schools in the Empire State, less than three score years ago. The present law, declared the resolutions, "is infidel socialism in its principles; unjust and oppressive in its operation; immoral in its tendency, irreligious in its consequences, and injurious to the cause of education; both by not possessing the proper requisites—and by destroying the harmony so necessary for its successful operation."[56]

Racial and religious opposition to the public school system during this period may be considered under one head, as these two forms of opposition usually went hand in hand. In New England, one nationality was predominant; differences in language did not complicate the situation. While many slightly different religious sects did spring up in New England, these were practically in accord in regard to the value and desirability of the maintenance of schools by the state rather than by the church.

[56] *New York Tribune*, September 26, 1850. Meeting held in Charton, Saratoga Co.

The scene is, therefore, shifted from New England to the Middle Region; and the most important and spectacular struggle of this nature occurred in Pennsylvania. In these states is found a heterogeneous population. In New York and Pennsylvania, for example, we see very clearly and distinctly, the clash of city against rural districts, agriculture against manufacture and commerce, nationality against nationality, and religion against religion. These two important states became the battle ground of interests, economic, racial and religious. They became the breeding grounds of political rings and bosses. Here we find the struggle for and against the public school system unrolled in all its severity and complexity. At present, we are concerned with and must examine only one phase; namely, that caused by the commingling in one commonwealth of different peoples possessing widely divergent ideas of life and religious beliefs. The antagonistic peoples are chiefly represented by the English on the one hand and the Germans and the Dutch on the other; the religious elements are the Calvinistic belief or some modification of it transplanted from New England, and the Quaker, Lutheran, or some allied sect.

As has already been mentioned, the attempt to carry out the provisions of the "pauper clause" in the constitution of the state of Pennsylvania, was not crowned with success. In the early part of 1834, an educational law was passed by the state legislature, with little consideration or opposition. Its provisions were not well understood at the time of its passage, and it proved to provide for a very cumbrous and unwieldy mechanism. The following quotation from a letter written by a member of the state legislature shows why the bill of 1833–1834 was carried with practically no opposition, and gives one reason for later opposition. "The bill reported by the joint committee of 1833–1834 was generally regarded as correct in principle, and, as members of either house were alike inexperienced, it was not much discussed, but was passed by a unanimous vote in the Senate and with but one dissenting vote in the House. Samuel Breck of the Senate, Chairman of the joint committee, was undoubtedly the author of the bill. He was a highly educated gentleman, past the meridian of life, who had never mixed much with the people living in country districts. Hence we cannot wonder that the main fault of this law, perhaps its only material fault, was the great amount of machinery required to carry it into effect."[57] This law provided for free schools for all in the districts accepting it. A state appropriation was provided to be distributed to those districts which would levy a local tax for the purpose of providing and maintaining free public schools. Districts not providing for local taxation received nothing from the state.[58]

The following quotations from Wickersham's admirable *History of Education in Pennsylvania,* give a vivid picture of the opposition which this unfortunate law stirred up and brought to the surface. "Of the 987 districts then in the State, 485 either voted outright against free schools or stubbornly took no action whatever in reference to the matter. In many districts the contest between those in favor of accepting the new law and those determined to reject it, became so bitter, that party and even church ties were for a time broken up, the rich arrayed themselves against the poor, and the business and social relations of whole neighborhoods were greatly dis-

[57] Quoted by Edmonds, *History of the Central High School of Phila.,* 21, foot note.

[58] Senator Breck was a New England man by birth. He was born in Boston, in 1771; and was at this time living near Philadelphia.

turbed. Cases are known in which father and son took different sides, and in certain districts an outspoken free school man was scarcely allowed to live in peace and transact his ordinary business."[59] The opposition was by no means entirely confined within certain religious denominations; but on another page the same author declared: "The new law (1833–1834) met with most favor in the northern counties. These had been settled principally by people from New England and New York, who had been accustomed to public schools and understood their advantages. It was comparatively well received in the counties west of the Alleghanies [*sic*], where a diversity in wealth had not yet bred distinctions of class, and where different nationalities and different religious denominations had become so thoroughly mixed as to recognize an educational interest in common. Opposition to it was most formidable in the southern, central, and southeastern portions of the State, and greatest of all in the counties and districts where the people were principally of German descent."[60] The Friends, Lutherans, the Reformed and Mennonites, where they were sufficiently numerous, usually had schools of their own and, as a rule, arrayed themselves against this law.[61] The free schools were called *"Zwing Schulen,"*—forced schools.

Of the Quakers and their view of education, Fiske writes:—"In spite of their liberalism, the Quakers attached far less importance to education than the Puritans of New England—Quakers, in studying the Bible depended upon their Inner Light rather than that critical interpretation of texts to which the orthodox Puritans attached so much importance."[62] In 1786 this prayer was

59 Wickersham, 318.
60 *Ibid.*, 318–19. See also Edmonds, 21.
61 *Ibid.*, 319.
62 *The Dutch and Quaker Colonies in America,* 2:320.

introduced into the litany of the Lutheran Church. "And since it has pleased Thee, chiefly by means of the Germans, to transform this state into a blooming garden, and the desert into a pleasant pasturage, help us not to deny our nation, but to endeavor that our youth may be so educated that German churches and schools may not only be sustained, but may attain a still more flourishing condition."[63] It was this conservatism which placed the Germans in the ranks of opposition to free public schools. "Many persons of German descent combated the free school idea because the instruction was to be given in the English language, and they feared that it would result in the displacement of their mother-tongue."[64] Hon. H. A. Muhlenberg in his frequently quoted letter to the workingmen of Philadelphia, (Jan. 1836) presents another reason for German opposition. "The Germans of our State are not opposed to education as such, but only to any system that to them seems to trench on their parental and natural rights." The opposition of the Germans was then, two-fold: their idea of an educational system was that of one dominated by the church and clergy, to this the public school stood directly opposed; and they feared anything which would tend to destroy the use of their language.

In the state of New York this phenomenon was less marked, but by no means absent. A newspaper correspondent, in 1850, wrote that objection to the free school law of 1849 came from "those who wished sectarian religious schools." Arguing from an economic point of view, he adds, "but, if in a school district of 200 inhabitants, we must have a Quaker, Presbyterian, Baptist, Methodist, Episcopalian and Roman Catholic school, it will be too

[63] Quoted by Kuhns, *German and Swiss Settlements in Penn.*, 117.
[64] Edmonds, 21.

expensive, and will cause education to be neglected."[65] Another account of the same period declares that, "religious prejudice was brought to bear on the side of popular ignorance with considerable effect."[66] In New York (1830–1860) "was being wrought out in the common school policy of the State the most difficult educational problem of the new Republic, the forming of a cosmopolitan people, representing all the political hostilities and obstinate religious differences of the past thousand years of European life, in one homogeneous civilization."[67]

It is unnecessary to dwell upon the retarding influence of hasty and ill-advised school legislation. Many bills were framed and passed which could not be carried into effect in an efficient manner. The result of ill-advised work of the friends of education was turned into a powerful weapon to be wielded by the hands of the enemies of free schools; and was utilized to turn many wavering ones in the direction of the opposition.

The opponents of the public school system who argued against it on the ground of its non-utility may be divided into two broad general classes: those honestly conservative members of the community who were unable to see wherein school instruction would benefit the children of the great mass of the people; and those who were opposed to the public school system for personal or mercenary reasons, but who used this argument as a cloak to conceal the real animus of their antagonism. A situation developed similar to that found in the early history of the steam or electric railroad, or of the introduction of gas lighting in cities. Many persons were truly apprehensive

[65] *New York Evening Post,* November 8, 1850.
[66] Editorial, *New York Tribune,* November 28, 1850.
[67] *Report of Commissioner of Education,* (1897–98), 464.

of the evils which they felt would follow in the wake of these, to them, startling and revolutionary innovations; others opposed their introduction because they were interested in enterprises which might be adversely affected by these new features of our industrial life.

An extract from John Randolph's speech before the Virginia Constitution Convention of 1829, illustrates in an extreme form, the view of the first class. "Among the strange notions which have been broached since I have been on the political theater, there is one which has lately seized the minds of men, that all things must be done for them by the government, and that they are to do nothing for themselves . . . Look at that ragged fellow staggering from the whiskey shop, and see the slattern who has gone to reclaim him; where are their children? Running about ragged, idle, ignorant, fit candidates for the penitentiary. Why is all this so? Ask the man and he will tell you, Oh! the government has undertaken to educate our children for us. It has given us a premium for idleness, and now I spend in liquor which I should otherwise be obliged to save, to pay for their schooling."[68] Mann speaks of secret opponents, and those who fought against the development of the Massachusetts school system from mercenary motives. He also mentions that many have no faith in the utility of education, and call it a Utopian scheme.[69]

The conservative opposition was particularly strong in the rural districts. Here the close connection between industry and home life was maintained long after it had vanished in the cities. School education is only one form of education. At this early period, school education consisted almost entirely of purely intellectual drill and dis-

[68] *Richmond Enquirer,* November 24, 1829.
[69] Mann, Horace, *Report of 1847, op. cit.,* 141.

cipline, and was limited to a very narrow range of subjects. The more modern idea of a broader and richer curriculum was not as yet even dreamed of; and indeed the time was not yet ripe for such a modification in the functions of the school.[70] The farming population could not see how education was to be of much benefit to their children; at least it was not clear to them that it was worth much sacrifice in the shape of higher taxes. The practical, hard-headed farmer could not see that much book-learning would help their children to earn their daily bread or enable them more easily to pay for a farm. The education they valued was obtained in the school of daily experience, on the farm itself. One of Pennsylvania's historians, in discussing the attitude of the farmers of that state on this subject, reveals the crux of the situation. "The main motive which led them to establish schools was not found in their daily occupations. Reading and sewing were valued for girls, and reading, writing and ciphering for boys, as necessary for life's duties, but the chief incentives to the employment of teachers must be sought in a realm outside of secular occupations. This was, in many cases, a religious motive."[71] To this must be added, at least in the case of the English-speaking farmer, the belief in the value of education in the formation of good citizens and, hence, in the preservation of free institutions.

Before passing to the consideration of the next argument, the following emphatic and sweeping charge is worthy of notice. At a meeting of teachers in Northampton, Massachusetts, as late as 1850, a Dr. Sylvester Graham "denounced the whole common school system as an evil,

[70] See two articles by the writer in *Engineering Magazine,* September, 1904, and *Education,* December, 1905.

[71] Jenkins, *Pennsylvania, Colonial and Federal,* 3:1, 2.

and said there was no safeguard for the young when away from the eyes of the parent, . . ."[72] This gentleman evidently wished for a return to the household form of education; the transformations wrought by industrial progress of the preceding thirty or forty years were not connected by him with a necessity for educational progress.

The antagonism between the public school system and the private schools and academies has been incidentally touched upon above.[73] In some states, the academies and public school societies were partially subsidized by the state. The proprietors of private schools felt that they ought not to be deprived of their opportunity to educate the young. No doubt they considered that they had a sort of vested interest which would be injured by the development of the public school system.[74]

The eighth and last argument against the public school system is nothing more or less than the use by the opposition of the second argument in favor of the system. What has been urged as a beneficent condition in society is now looked upon with alarm. The working classes and the frontiersman hailed equality and the lowering of social barriers as undisguised blessings. But certain elements in the community opposed the public school, because it tended to strengthen the spirit of democracy. "It is curious to see how long the higher social circles of the commercial towns,—Boston, Salem, and Newburyport—clung to the old traditions, and how they resisted the encroachments of that leveling spirit which would break down the old social barriers. Thus in Newburyport, in 1790, when it was proposed to open primary schools for

[72] *New York Evening Post,* August 20, 1850.

[73] Second argument in favor of public schools.

[74] See Steiner, *History of Education in Maryland,* 62 *et seq.*

girls at public expense, the school committee of clergymen, doctors, squires, and captains recommended that all girls who attended these schools should be considered as recipients of public charity. This the town rejected."[75] Niles in an editorial states that a man, "then a senator of the United States, declared, in my presence, and many other times in the presence of others, that the government could never be properly administered until the laboring classes were reduced to a livelihood on herrings and potatoes."[76]

[75] Martin, *Evolution of the Mass. Public School System,* 143.
[76] *Niles' Register,* (1816), 2:2.

5. The Alignment of Interests

The story of the development of our tariff system, for example, is the history of a struggle between different interests and sections within the United States as a whole; likewise our educational advance, indirectly modified by the influence of progress in one state upon that in another, was, and is, the resultant of the conflict of interests—economic, social, religious and racial—within the different states. The bitterness of the struggle is augmented where great diversity of interests exist. We must look, as in the study of our tariff history, to the motives which actuated groups of men, rather than particular men. The study of the actual alignment of interests has, of course, been to some extent anticipated in the last chapter. In studying these forces or influences we must consider them as abstract and impersonal. A given individual may be influenced by many more or less conflicting and antagonistic interests and desires. Imagine, for instance, a German-Lutheran wage-earner and non-taxpayer living in a city; his racial and religious bias would tend to produce a somewhat different attitude on the subject of free education from that which his economic and occupational interests would tend to create. In other words, the individual is a focus of many more or less conflicting emotions, demands and ideals. Religious belief and inherited traits, particularly during a period of rapid industrial and social modification, often stand in opposition to the influence of occupational or economic forces. The individual on account of his membership in conflicting groups may be first on one side and then on the other. His allegiance is determined by the strength of contending motives, and is necessarily altered by changes in his social environment, his occupation, economic environment, and so on through a long list. The individual is more or less submerged in the mass. His views are biased and colored by the aims and ideals of the class to which he belongs, or the interests which he represents.

The following classification of interests acting for and against the development of a system of tax-supported public schools may be of assistance.

For	*Against, or lukewarm;*
Men considered as:	Men considered as:
Citizens of the Republic.	Residents of rural districts.
Workingmen.	Tax-payers.
Non-tax-payers.	Members of exclusive or ultra conservative classes.
Calvinists.	Lutherans, Quakers, etc.
Residents of cities.	Possessing a mother tongue other than English.
	Proprietors of Private Schools.

Such an analysis does not signify that all workingmen were favorable to the public schools, or that all Germans, for example, were opposed to them. It indicates that the workingmen, as a class during this period, stood for better educational facilities, and that the Germans, in the main, were unfriendly to an institution which seemed to threaten the continuation of the use of their mother tongue.

In the American nation which had recently achieved independence after a long and costly struggle, and had established a republican form of government, the good of the republic became almost a religion to the mass of the people. Pleas for education as the cornerstone upon which good citizenship rests, strengthened because of the rising tide of foreign immigration, exercised a powerful influence. Practically every argument considered, in the last chapter, which was favorable to education appealed to the man as a citizen, and three (2, 5 and 6) of the opposing arguments also favorably impressed him. The citizens' belief in free institutions and in the desirability or the necessity of education in order to maintain them was balanced against the danger of infringing upon the liberty and the rights of the individual, through compulsory taxation for educational purposes. The arguments which urged that education diminished crime and poverty, and increased production, decreased the opposition of the taxpayer. Where the numerical strength of a religious sect, in a given district, was not sufficient to warrant the establishment of sectarian schools, the effect was, as a rule, to reduce the opposition to the public schools on the part of the members of sects who were, under other conditions, strongly arrayed against it. Similarly, the strength of the individual opposition of non-English-speaking settlers was diminished wherever the concentration of this class of people was not particularly marked. It is perhaps unnecessary to consider further the position taken by different interests, except that of the cities and rural districts, and that of the workingmen.

As early as 1799, the Mechanics' Association of Providence made a vigorous demand for a system of public schools. In the same year the legislature of Rhode Island enacted a local option school law; but only Providence availed itself of the law, and it was repealed by the votes of the remainder of the state in 1803.[1] Three decades

[1] Mayo, *Rep't of Com. of Education,* 1896–97, 784 *et seq.*

later, in the fall of 1829, the interest of workingmen in the question of public education suddenly rose to a fever heat, and continued unabated during 1830. From that time it seemed gradually to diminish and in the forties very little is heard about education from the spokesman of the workers.[2] They were, during this later period, more interested in other pressing problems, of which the public land question was perhaps the most important. This ebb in the sentiment favoring public education appears to be due, in part, to the fact that the workers came to realize that education was not a panacea for all social ills; and to be partly due to the improvement in the school system during the decade of the thirties. That the workers remained firm believers in the desirability of a free school is, however, adequately proven by the decisive referendum vote in New York State in 1850.[3]

Nevertheless, there is adequate evidence that the Workingmen's parties of Philadelphia and New York, although they took up education as the chief plank in their platform, did not originate in a demand for better educational facilities for the masses.[4] That was a later de-

[2] When the *Working Man's Advocate* (N. Y.), edited by Geo. H. Evans, first appeared on October 31, 1829, it was wildly enthusiastic on the subject of education. Evans declared that this was the one measure which would regenerate society. But when, after the publication had been discontinued for several years, a new series appeared (1844) under the joint editorship of Evans and John Windt, other problems attracted the editors' attention.

[3] See latter part of this chapter.

[4] At a meeting of "mechanics and other workingmen" held in April, 1829, a committee of fifty was appointed to draft resolutions to be read at a later meeting. On October 19, 1829, this committee made its report. While recognizing the fundamental importance of education they held that other reforms must first be adopted. This report may be found in the first issue of the *Working Man's Advocate,* October 31, 1829. The preamble of the Mechanic's Union of

velopment. It was taken up at a time when agitation was rampant. The workers felt that they were suffering from grievious [*sic*] ills; and they were looking for a remedy. For years it had been impressed upon the public that education made for equality; that it was a prime essential in a free country. In both New York and Pennsylvania the governors' messages had repeatedly heralded this opinion. Nicholas Biddle in 1810 had voiced this sentiment in an official report to the legislature of Pennsylvania.[5] New England men, like James G. Carter, had been faithfully preaching the gospel of education. The trustees of the Public School Society, in a widely circulated report, had declared that "those who are without education must always be a degraded caste."[6] Finally came men like Robert Dale Owen and Geo. H. Evans teaching a still more radical doctrine as to the efficacy and need of better educational facilities.

Suddenly the workers became enthused on the subject. It spread like wildfire. Practically every workingmen's meeting from Albany to Wilmington and Charleston took up the cry; for one or two years few sets of resolu-

---

Trade Associations of Philadelphia (1828) does not mention the subject of education, but does demand increased leisure time. See the *Mechanics' Free Press,* October 25, 1828. Similar sentiments are found in "An Address to the Journeymen House Carpenters of Philadelphia" in *Mechanics' Free Press,* June 14, 1829. The Workingmen's Party in New York City has been said to have originated as the result of a demand for a mechanic's lien law. See Hammond, *Political History of New York,* 2: 330; and Jenkins, J. S., *History of Political Parties in New York,* 1:369. But the first impulse seems to have been due to a demand for a greater amount of leisure time. See *Morning Courier,* (N. Y.), April 25, 1829 and April 30, 1829.

[5] Printed in full in the *Working Man's Advocate,* April 3, 1830; from the *Mechanics' Free Press,* (Phila).

[6] 5,000 copies of this "Address to the Public" were printed and distributed February, 1829. Printed in full in Bourne's *History of the Public School Society of N. Y.,* 110–118.

tions were passed in workingmen's meetings which did not give a prominent place to a demand for educational reforms. When, in the period 1833 to 1836, union organization supplants the loose party associations, the demand is still continued; but the question of wages becomes uppermost. In Boston, where the school system was better organized than elsewhere, the educational demand is not so prominent. In Rhode Island, the suffrage question overshadowed all else in the minds of the workingmen.

In order to show the attitude of the wage earners, a few typical resolutions and declarations from various cities will be selected from the mass of such material. At a meeting of workingmen held in New York City in November, 1829, resolutions were adopted which read in part as follows: "Resolved, that the most grievous species of inequality is that produced by inequality in education, and that a national system of education and guardianship which shall furnish to all children of the land, equal food, clothing and instruction at the public expense is the only effectual remedy for this and for almost every other species of injustice. Resolved, that all other modes of reform are, compared to this, particular, inefficient, or trifling."[7] Again among the resolutions adopted by a "General Meeting of Mechanics and Working Men" of New York City, held December 29, 1829, are found the following: "Resolved, that next to life and liberty, we consider education the greatest blessing bestowed upon mankind. Resolved, that the public funds should be appropriated (to a reasonable extent) to the purpose of education upon a regular system that shall insure the opportunity to every individual of obtaining a competent education before he shall have arrived at the age of ma-

[7] *Free Enquirer*, (N. Y.), November 7, 1829, 15.

turity."[8] In an official communication from the Painters' Society of the City and County of New York to the "Association for the Protection of Industry and the Promotion of National Education," is found this statement of opinion; "We are therefore of opinion . . . that the State should furnish throughout the land, at public expense, state institutions, where every young citizen should be educated and maintained from youth to manhood, and where each should obtain (besides the various branches of a liberal education) a competent knowledge, of at least one trade or occupation, by which even while completing his education, he may earn his living."[9]

A workingmen's meeting in Philadelphia on September 26, 1829, adopted a preamble which contained the following clause: "No system of education, which a freeman can accept, has yet been established for the poor; whilst thousands of dollars of the public money have been appropriated for building colleges and academies for the rich."[10] "The determined stand taken by the productive classes of the community of the city and county of Philadelphia, and in many other sections of the Union, to accomplish the important object of a general and equal system, is beheld with emotions of heartfelt pleasure by every friend of liberty."[11] At New Castle, Delaware, in 1830, an Association of Workingmen was formed. In the preamble of their constitution they endorsed this sentiment; "Let us unite at the polls and give our votes to no candidate who is not pledged to support a rational system of education to be paid for out

[8] *Working Man's Advocate,* January 16, 1830.

[9] *Free Enquirer,* January 9, 1830, 83.

[10] *Working Man's Advocate,* October 31, 1829. For other Pennsylvania meetings, *ibid.*, February 13, 1830.

[11] Quoted, *ibid.,* January 30, 1830, from *Mechanics' Free Press*

of the public funds, and to further a rightful protection to the laborer."[12]

At an adjourned meeting of "Workingmen, Mechanics, and others friendly to their interests," held in Boston, August 17, 1830, it was resolved, "that the establishment of a liberal system of education, attainable by all, should be among the first efforts of every lawgiver who desires the continuance of our national independence."[13] In its editorial address the *Workingmen's Advocate and Practical Politician* (Boston) used the same phraseology regarding the duties of lawgivers.[14] The committee on education appointed at a workingmen's convention held in Boston, October 2, 1833, recommended, in addition to facilities for elementary education, lectures to adults on political economy, and a general system of education by means of manual labor schools "free to all, at the expense of each State." It was also suggested that ministers ought "to enlighten the people on their true temporal interests."[15] In an oration delivered before an association of trade unions in Boston, on July 4, 1834, Frederick Robinson declared: "We are yet but a half-educated and half-civilized people. The few are educated in one-half their faculties, and the people in the other half. The many have been obliged to devote their whole time to bodily labor, while the powers of mind have been almost wholly neglected."[16] Thus, he anticipated the more recent advocates of manual training. At a banquet given

[12] Quoted, McMaster, *Acquisition of Political, Social and Industrial Rights,* 107. See also, *Delaware Free Press,* May 22, 1830.

[13] *Boston Courier,* August 28, 1830.

[14] Quoted, *Boston Courier,* March 11, 1831.

[15] *Proceedings of the Working Men's Convention.* Pamphlet in Atheneum library.

[16] Rogers, E. H., *Minority Rep't of Commissioners on Hours of Labor. Mass. House Bill, No. 4, 1867.*

in the evening of the same day, one of the toasts was, "Manual labor schools—The salvation of our institutions and the hope of the children of the poor."[17]

A committee from the General Trades Union of Cincinnati, Ohio, issued in 1836 an "Appeal to the Working Men of the West," in which they state that their efforts will be directed toward elevating the condition of the "Working Man," and toward obtaining a "National System of Education."[18] In 1835, the workingmen of Washington in an enumeration of their demands, stated; "We ask for a universal system of education; for the abolishment of monopolies; for the abolishment of imprisonment for debt; and for a just representation of all interests. These are the objects we ask, and all we ask. The charges that are made against us of agrarianism and a desire to strip from the rich the possessions they have acquired, or which have descended to them by inheritance, is as false as the spirit is despicable that makes the charge."[19] In the first number of a western labor paper, the editor writes, "But what shall claim our particular attention will be a system of Public, Republican, Scientific, Practical Education for the Poor as well as for the Rich, looking to the Treasury of the Nation for a part of the surplus revenue, to carry it into effect."[20] *The National Laborer* (Philadelphia) published by the "Workingmen's National Society for the Diffusion of Useful Knowledge," informed the public that it would "advo-

[17] *Ibid.*

[18] *The Washingtonian,* August 8, 1836, 2.

[19] *Address to the Mechanics of the District of Columbia,* issued by the Trades Union of the D. of C. Pamphlet in the Library of Congress.

[20] *The Union and Mechanics' and Working Men's Advocate,* Indianapolis, Ind. Quoted in *Working Man's Advocate,* June 11, 1831, 3.

cate the establishment of a Universal Republican System of Education, knowing that to a want of knowledge alone may be ascribed all the evils which infest society, and which bear particularly heavy on the productive classes."[21]

In 1830 the "Farmers', Mechanicks' and Workingmen's" party of New York held a state convention at Salina, and nominated Erastus Root for Governor. Among others, the convention gave its adherence to the following resolution, "Resolved, that a system of education more universal in its effects, is practicable, so that no child in the republick, however poor, should grow up without an opportunity to acquire at least a competent English education; and that the system should be adapted to the condition of the poor both in the city and country."[22] The Equal Rights party of the city and county of New York, which was in a measure the successor of the Workingmen's party, in 1837 pledged itself "to procure a more extended, equal and convenient system of Common School Instruction."[23] The letter of Hon. H. A. Muhlenberg to the workingmen of Philadelphia[24] clearly indicates that the workingmen of that city were deeply interested in education, in 1834–1836; and also it is good evidence that they were an important political factor at that time.

The foregoing, together with statements in preceding chapters, is sufficient to establish the fact that the workingmen of the country were much alive to the benefits of a system of public schools, and that their influence was an important factor in hastening the development of the

21 *National Laborer,* March 26, 1836, I, No. 1.

22 *The Craftsman,* Rochester, September 4, 1830.

23 *Farmer's and Mechanics' Journal,* Alexander, N. Y., November 4, 1837.

24 Quoted in ch. 4.

system. This item in the program of the labor movement of the first half of last century is now generally accepted throughout the United States, and by all classes. The progress of the world has been, for centuries, toward the betterment of the working classes; it seems reasonable, therefore, to argue *a priori* that, if progress continues, the chief items in the program of the working people and non-property owners of one generation will be accepted in the next, by society as a whole. As long as progress means the uplift of the workers, so long will their program rather than that of the business or professional man represent progress. The latter acts as a fly-wheel which steadies progress, and prevents disaster; but they stand for controlling or modifying, not impelling, forces. This view is particularly illuminating in studying the educational development of our period. In the cities, a large proportion of the people were workingmen and small taxpayers; and in the cities the need of educational facilities was most clearly urgent; and better opportunities were offered for carrying on an agitation. But the workingmen's zeal in the cause of universal education came down to him from the traditions and experience of the past; and was kept alive and made more intense by the labors and exhortations of the leaders of the humanitarian movement.

With the development of the factory system, the problem of child labor assumes a threatening form on the horizon of the educational and industrial world. Before the factory era, at certain periods of the year there was little work for the children at home. This time was utilized, in many sections, for school work. With the rise of the cities and the growth of factories, the children began to be sent out of the home to work. Industry lost much of its seasonal character; and, if the children were sent to school, a reduction of the family income was, apparently, the direct and measurable result. The question of education now became immediately and directly a factor in the household economy of the workingman. The inevitable tendency, in many instances, was to slight education, to mortgage the future for the present; immediate concrete earnings looked larger and more inviting than future indefinite opportunities for the children of the family. The interests of the mill-owner and of the poor, lazy, or short-sighted workman were united as to the desirability of child labor. The phenomenon of child-labor caused a certain class of workingmen to become less insistent in their demands for educational facilities. Child-labor in factories spelled lack of education for the workers. Seth Luther in drawing his gloomy picture of the evils of child-labor and of excessively long hours of work, compared the position of the workingmen to the situation of a horse whose master was asked if he ever fed him. "Fed him, now that's a good 'un; why he's got a bushel and a half of oats at home, only he 'aint [*sic*] got no time to eat 'um."[25] This told the story of the workingman's opportunity to get an education in the mill town of New England in the thirties.

The influence of prosperity and demand for child workers was disastrous to school attendance. For example, in 1820, over 5,000 pupils were on the rolls of the public schools of Philadelphia.[26] But as the country began to recover from the effects of the crisis of 1819, the demand for child labor increased with the result that in 1821 less than 3,000 were in the schools of that city; and the school authorities called for legislative action. "In

[25] Address, *Education of Workingmen,* (1832).

[26] *Third Annual Rep't of Controllers of Public Schools of the First School District of the State of Pennsylvania,* 4. Quoted McMaster, 5: 359.

1822 the attendance was 450 less than in 1821, and in 1823 was less than half what it had been in 1820."[27] Nearly a score of years later, the following testimony was given as to child-labor in Connecticut. "The comparative cheapness of the labor of females, and of children, where it can be resorted to at all, has led to its excessive introduction into factories, to the exclusion as far as possible, of the more costly labor of men. . . . One thing is clear from the experience of the past, both at home and abroad, that about such establishments will always be gathered a large number of parents, who either from defective education in themselves, or from the pressure of immediate want, or from the selfishness which is fostered by finding profitable employment for their children do not avail themselves" of the advantages of free schools.[28] Where the factory system exists with its regularity of operation throughout the year, the maintenance of a public school system is not alone sufficient. It must be supplemented by laws restricting child-labor and by compulsory education laws. Such enactments are difficult of passage, in many cases, because of the attitude of the workingman himself, particularly where organized labor is not strong. In certain states where manufacture is just springing into prominence and importance, the problem which faced New England three-quarters of a century ago is now being re-solved. In several of the southern states which are now entering the industrial field, the evils of child-labor are great,—equal to those of which Luther so bitterly complained. One recent observer remarks, "the interest of the cracker, the preacher, the

[27] McMaster, 5:360.

[28] *First Annual Rep't of the Sec. (Henry Barnard) of the Board of Common School Commissioners of Conn.,* May, 1839. Quoted in *Conn. Common School Journal,* 1:166.

overseer, the superintendent, the president, and the stockholder are so involved that they cannot see the truth."[29] The individual workingman is a prey to conflicting interests in regard to the question of educating his children; but his organization now, as in the earlier period, stands for education and against child labor which deprives the child of its opportunity to attend school, or to live the normal, healthy life of a child.

This period which was distinguished by the development of the industrial town, marks the rise of the urban school. The city then assumed the educational leadership; development in education during the nineteenth century was chiefly directed and conditioned by the needs of urban life and by the changes in industrial methods. Town and city life coupled with the development of the factory system or of an intensified system of domestic industry, deprived the child of opportunity for home instruction as to the practical affairs of life, and removed him from contact with nature and diversified industry. The city child lived in crowded quarters, and was forced constantly to associate with a heterogeneous mass of youngsters. He could work as a wage-earner outside or even inside the home, go to school, or run the streets. Concentration of population apparently multiplied the evils of ignorance and poverty; division of labor and increasing specialization of industry tended to deprive the child of invaluable training in regularity and industry. It was assumed by the leaders of the educational renaissance that intellectual education alone would remedy the difficulty. The effect of changed environment and modified home conditions due to growth of cities and innovations in industry was not as yet understood. The manual labor schools which flourished for

[29] Hubbard, *American Federationist,* April, 1905.

a short space of time were concrete results of a partial recognition of the necessity for a close connection between intellectual and manual labor; but the time was not yet ripe. City life and industrial specialization had not as yet assumed sufficient importance in our national life. Thirty or forty years after the close of our period came the triumph of the principle of manual training, although, even today, many intelligent persons deny or minimize its educational value. In the thirties, purely intellectual education was advocated, except by the communists, as the magic wand which would arrest the progress of the wave of juvenile crime, transform the weak and erring boy into the good citizen, perpetuate the republic, train the efficient worker, and instill the ideals of America into the child of the immigrant.

In the cities the effects of the new industrial, home and social life which the industrial evolution of this period ushered in, were first and most markedly felt. Reformers and the mass of the people of the cities turned with an almost child-like faith to the school,—the common school of the three R's. This was perhaps a groping in the dark, a failure to recognize changing conditions, a measurement of present necessities according to worn-out and obsolete standards; but it led to a step in advance. We of today know that the educators of that day did not grasp the significance of the industrial evolution going on before their eyes; but we are repeating the blunder year after year. Educational progress is still lagging far behind industrial advance. The modern movement for free public schools originated in the cities; and improvements in educational methods and curricula first find a place in the city schools, because here the necessity is greatest and most noticeable. Indeed, the educational conservatism and apathy of the rural districts during the period (1820–1850) is accounted for chiefly by two circumstances. The industrial changes did not vitally effect [*sic*] the industrial and home life of the farmer of this period; and in the country nearly every man paid direct taxes. The added expense of schools, or of improvements in schools, was visible to all and felt by all. Another phenomenon which tended to increase the conservatism of the rural population in New England is familiar to the student of the more recent period of our national life, namely, the drawing of the best blood of the rural districts into the cities or toward the West.[30] This migration began early to affect the attitude of the rural districts of Massachusetts, Connecticut and Rhode Island as to educational advance; and by 1850, its effect was not negligible in the state of New York. In the Pennsylvania contest of 1834 and 1835, however, this phenomenon need not be considered; and in Ohio, Indiana, and Illinois up to the end of the period, the pioneer element was still predominant in the rural districts.

The antagonism of the rural districts of Rhode Island to the law of 1799–1800, and of those of Massachusetts to the laws of 1826 and 1836, have already been mentioned.[31] In Pennsylvania, Philadelphia provided for practically free schools at public expense several years before the passage of the free school law of 1834. But it is to New York that we must turn for the most clear-cut and spectacular exhibition of the antagonism between urban and rural districts on the question of free tax-supported schools. In March, 1849, the New York Legislature passed an "Act establishing free schools throughout the State." These schools were to be free to all children between the ages of five and twenty-one. Local

[30] See Martin, *Evolution of the Mass. Public School System,* 203.
[31] See also the section on "The South" in ch. 6.

taxation was authorized to supplement the state tax. A referendum was granted; and the vote stood 249,872 for, and 91,951 against, the enactment of such a law. In New York county, the vote was 21,052, in favor of; against 1,313; in Richmond county, 1,437 to 22 respectively; and in Kings county, 8,549 to 159. The foregoing three counties were strictly urban counties, including and surrounding New York City and Brooklyn. Albany county, containing the city of Albany, gave 8,604 votes for, and 1,806 against, the proposed law; Erie county, containing the city of Buffalo, 8,800 to 1,542 respectively. Only four counties gave majorities against the bill: these were the rural counties of Tompkins, Chenango, Cortland, and Otsega.[32] As soon as the attempt to put the law into actual operation was made, however, great hostility was manifested.

In the next year, 1850, the question of the repeal of the law was referred to the people. Forty-two out of a total of fifty-nine counties now favored the repeal; but the majority given by the seventeen was sufficiently large to prevent this retrograde step. The vote was 209,346 against, and 184,308 for, the repeal. The seventeen counties which were against the repeal are the following: Albany, Columbia, Dutchess, Erie, Kings, Montgomery, New York, Onondaga, Putnam, Queens, Renssalaer [*sic*], Richmond, Rockland, Schenectady, Seneca, Ulster and Westchester.[33] New York, Kings, Queens, and Richmond counties included New York City, Brooklyn and suburbs; Albany county, the city of Albany; Erie county, the city of Buffalo; Renssalaer [*sic*] county, the city of Troy; Schenectady county, the city of Schenectady; Onon-

[32] Randall, *History of the Common School System of N. Y.*, 74 *et seq.*

[33] *Ibid.*

dago [*sic*] county, the city of Syracuse; and Columbia, Dutchess, Putnam, Rockland, Ulster and Westchester counties border on the Hudson river, and lie between New York and Albany. The voice of the cities was unmistakable. Although the legislature did not fully carry out the will of the majority as represented by this referendum, and although the rate bill in a modified form was not finally abolished until several years later, this vote may be said to have definitely settled the matter of tax-supported schools in the state of New York. *The New York Tribune,* in commenting on this referendum, said: "the cities have fairly tried free schools as the country has not; our approval of them is founded on knowledge, while the country's hostility is in good part founded on prejudice."[34]

Before the eye and the mind are distracted by the details which a study of the different states will present, let us examine briefly the outline picture which is now before us. The second great period in our educational development follows closely upon the rapid growth of industrial centers, the increase of manufacture, and of mutual interdependence due in this case to the birth of the modern factory system and the specialization of industry. Preceding the educational revival of the second quarter of the nineteenth century the prevailing type of school was rural rather than urban. Horace Mann "stands in history as the representative of the urban school." It is important to notice that at the moment when the theories of natural rights, *laissez faire,* individualism, are apparently at high-water mark, we find a growing demand for protection for the manufacturing classes and for tax-supported free schools for all classes, and an increasing tendency away from an extremely de-

[34] Editorial, *N. Y. Tribune,* November 28, 1850.

centralized administrative system. These three important manifestations of this period of social unrest are not mutually unrelated phenomena. They are the natural fruit of specialization and concentration of industry and of the development of improved methods of transportation; in short, of the introduction of modern industrial and commercial methods. They mark the widening and intensifying of the sphere of common interests. Urban communities demand an increase in collective activity over that required by rural districts.

The religious motive for the support of the common schools which had been predominant in colonial times, has now dropped out of sight. With the growing heterogeneity of population, the elements which fostered the school system in the early history of New England lost interest, and turned to the private schools. This period (1820–1850) marks the rise of the influence of manufacturing interests and of the city in the affairs of the nation. The cities and the workingmen looked to economic, civic and ethical motives. The prevention of class differentiation and the preservation of free institutions are the two arguments in which these two overlapping elements of our population saw the chief justification of tax-supported schools. The elements of our population whose agitation and political power forced the general acceptance of the doctrine of free education for all, were pushed to the front and made powerful factors in American life as a result of mechanical inventions and industrial progress. The visible and honored leaders were humanitarians whose zeal was developed by a genuine desire to alleviate the suffering and misery which the rapid growth of towns, workshops and factories was producing. The point which this analysis throws into clear view is one which has been, hitherto, almost uniformly overlooked or neglected, namely, that the real underlying forces with which we are chiefly concerned are industrial. Educational history during the first half of the nineteenth century must be studied by the aid of the light given us by industrial history. The inventor and the *entrepreneur* guided the steps of the educator and the legislator.

In short, the power loom, the slide-rest, steam and water power, the canal, the railroad and the blast furnace have increased the size and the importance of the cities, added to the numbers who toil for wages and built up an important manufacturing interest. The consequent displacement of the political and social center of gravity developed that unique and powerful, although not numerically strong, class called humanitarians. The frontier has placed the ballot in the hands of the adult white male population; and the increasing mobility of population has softened the animosities of sectarian and racial differences. Directed and aided by the humanitarian leaders, the workingmen and the cities have effectively used the weapon placed in their hands by the men of the frontier. The agitation for tax-supported schools which gradually acquired strength during the first fifteen years of the period, came to fruition during the latter decade and a half. The educational ideal of the Puritan has receded into the background, and a new democratic one conceived during this period of unrest and social flux, has replaced it. Each section or each state has its own peculiar trend of industrial and educational advance. In order to complete the picture and to note whether the details harmonize with the outlines already sketched, a detailed study of several representative states must be undertaken.

6. Progress in Different States

MASSACHUSETTS

In Massachusetts, as we have seen, the principle of tax-supported schools was firmly established. It came down from the act of 1647. In this state and in Connecticut, the old traditions as to education never completely lost their hold. There was, however, a modification in regard to the relation of the state to education. The early New England statutes emphasized the right of the state to compel the father to provide education for his children. The view which was generally accepted before the end of this period 1820–1850, placed the emphasis upon the duties of the state. The latter should not only demand the education of all children; but must also provide schools and teachers.[1] The following newspaper clipping gives an idea of the condition of the schools of Boston at the end of the first decade of our period. "The system of education here, supported from the municipal treasury, takes the child at four years of age, and carries it through a course of education, till it is fourteen, or older if a pupil at the Latin or High School. The range of instruction is from the A, of the alphabet, through the sciences, and to a knowledge of the Greek and Latin languages. The number of Public Schools in Boston is 68 . . . and the estimated expense, for the current year, is $52,500. The assumption of this duty by the city, secures

[1] Perrin, *Compulsory Education.* (Univ. of Chicago, 1896.)

the tuition of all children, while it relieves parents from much direct care and expense. It increases the taxes, but the addition to rate-bill is inconsiderable, compared with what the preceptor's charges would be against the parents."[2]

The struggle for better education in Massachusetts was twofold: centralization of authority in order to overcome the glaring evils of the district system, and the establishment of free public high schools. One serious obstacle standing in the way of the improvement in the schools of Massachusetts was alleged to be "the little interest taken by the most enlightened part of the community . . . in the condition of the common schools, from the circumstances that their own children are receiving education in private schools at their own expense."[3] A state of affairs developed similar to that which is found where various religious denominations support schools of their own. The influence of the private schools of this state during the twenties and thirties was considerable. "The amount paid for tuition in private schools, for one-sixth of the children of the state, is $328,000; while the amount raised by taxes for the education of the other five-sixths in public schools is $465,000, and the amount voluntarily contributed to the public schools is $48,000."[4] "The district school of the central village . . . often is . . . the poorest in the whole territory."[5] In 1830 returns from 131 towns in Massachusetts, showed that the annual amount paid in those towns for public schools was $170,342.96; and the number of pupils, 12,393.[6] There was

[2] *New England Palladium and Commercial Advertiser,* July 10, 1829.

[3] *North American Review,* (1838), 47:303.

[4] *Ibid.,* 304.

[5] *Ibid.,* 305.

[6] *Niles' Register,* 38:401.

urgent need of improving the public schools; but the friends of the private schools were hostile and powerful.

The fight which centered around the legalizing of the high school presented many features similar to those found in New York and Pennsylvania in regard to the tax-supported elementary school. The opposition between rural and urban districts was clearly marked; and the rural forces were reinforced by the friends of the private schools. "In towns containing a village center, growing populous under the new order of things, a struggle began between the village and the outskirts, often protracted for years. The movement for the town high school was in most cases an occasion for an annual tug of war."[7] The law of 1826 made obligatory upon the towns of Massachusetts, the establishment of a high school, to be open ten months in the year. The two elements of opposition soon succeeded in securing a partial repeal of the act. In 1836, the law was reenacted in its original form; but again in 1840, it was practically repealed. In 1848, however, it was again placed upon the statute books.[8]

The recognition of the growing evils of child labor in factories found expression in the law which went into effect April 1, 1837. The law required three months schooling in the twelve months preceding the child's employment by a manufacturing establishment. Of its enforcement, Horace Mann wrote; "Comparatively speaking there seems to have been far greater disregard of the law by private individuals and by small corporations, especially where the premises are rented from year to year, or from term to term, than by the owners and agents of

[7] Martin, *Evolution of the Mass. Common School System,* 203.
[8] *Ibid.,* 198.

large establishments."[9] In general, a like situation obtains today in regard to apprenticeship. The larger establishments are most keenly alive to the desirability of the establishment of systems of apprenticeship.

The peculiar and distinctive feature of the development of the school system of Massachusetts is the strength of tradition and habit. Conservatism and radicalism in education joined hands on the proposition that free tax-supported elementary schools were desirable. The habit of paying taxes for the support of public schools was formed and fixed. Here the past for other reasons than those advanced by the then present, and acting according to different motives from those which actuated the men of the time under consideration, had removed the greatest obstacle in the path of educational evolution in this period.

CONNECTICUT

The development of the Connecticut school system up to 1800 was not greatly dissimilar from that of Massachusetts; and the industrial development during our period was similar in these two New England states. The distinctive feature in Connecticut seems to be her large educational fund. Like Massachusetts, she acquiesced in the proposition of supporting schools through taxation, until the fund derived from the sale of lands practically removed the necessity of local taxation. While in 1800 the school system of Connecticut was equal, if not superior, to that of Massachusetts; in 1850 the latter state was unquestionably in advance educationally of her sister state.

[9] Mann, *Report for 1839* in *Life and Works of H. Mann,* 3:5.

"Prior to 1795, with the exception of the proceeds ot the sale of seven new townships in the Western part of this state [Connecticut] in 1733 and certain sums of money due on excise on goods in 1765, which were divided among the towns, and the interest of the same, appropriated forever, to the support of the Common Schools, the expense of public schools fell upon the inhabitants of the town, or upon the parents and guardians of the children who attended them. Up to this time it was rare to meet with a native of Connecticut who could not read or write, so that the provisions thus made, and the care with which the money was applied, met the wants of the community. In 1795, the avails of the sale of Western land, now forming part of Ohio, amounting to $1,200,000 was forever appropriated to the support of Common Schools, and in 1818, this legislative distinction was confirmed, with the sanction of Constitutional provision."[10] But the writer complains of the "criminal apathy" regarding the public schools, and of the increase of private schools, although at that time (1838), the school fund amounted to nearly $2,000,000.

Testimony is not lacking to prove that the existence of this unusually large school fund, produced a feeling of apathy in regard to public education in Connecticut, and that, unfortunately, it undermined the habit, which was formed during the early colonial period, of supporting the public schools through direct local taxation. An apparently beneficent influence soon proved to be detrimental. By 1838, it was recorded that "the schools had ceased to command the confidence of many intelligent citizens, and were no longer the main reliance of the whole community for elementary instruction. . . . Tax-

[10] *Report of the Joint Select Committee on Common Schools* in *Conn. Com. School Journ.*, 1838, 1:2–3.

ation for school purposes had not only ceased to be the cheerful habit of the people, but was regarded as something foreign and anti-democratic. The supervision of the schools had become in most societies a mere formality . . . and the whole system seemed struck with paralysis."[11] An article in the *North American Review* for April, 1823, states: "Taxation for schools being infrequent, must be borne with impatience; and if some school societies increase the school money by tax, the practice is gradually discontinued, and will soon cease entirely. As to time then, we do not find that anything has been gained by the school from the operation of the fund. If some schools continue longer, each year, others are brought sooner to a close, the amount of time, through the whole, being not materially varied."[12] A committee of citizens of New Jersey investigated the Connecticut system in 1828; and reported "that the Connecticut system does produce the result of repressing the liberality of the people toward this object of benevolence,[13] and leads them into the habit of relying upon the public money, to the neglect of education in most of their districts, during a considerable part of the year, we have the best reasons for believing."[14]

In 1837, Henry Barnard estimated that 10,000 children of the rich and educated were receiving good instruction in private schools at an expense greater than that appropriated for the other 60,000 or 70,000 children of the state.[15]

[11] *Barnard's Journal*, (1858), 5:154.

[12] Quoted *Barnard's Journal*, (1858), 5:126. For amount of annual dividends from school fund, see *ibid.*, 6:425; 1820, $58,439.36; 1850, $136,505.50.

[13] The use of the word "benevolence" should be noticed.

[14] *Barnard's Journal*, 5:133.

[15] *Ibid.*, 5:153.

As early as 1813, a law was enacted requiring the proprietors of manufacturing establishments to see that the children employed by them were instructed in reading, writing and arithmetic; "and that due attention was paid to their morals."[16] But in the first report of the newly formed Board of Commissioners of Common Schools, Mr. Barnard complains that this law is not well enforced. "It will be but poor glory for Connecticut to be able to point to her populous and industrious manufacturing villages as the workshops of the Union, . . . if they are also to become blots upon her intellectual and moral character."[17] The same writer stated that non-attendance upon any school in the cities was confined chiefly to four classes. (a) "The children of the reckless, the vicious, and the intemperate," . . . not readily amenable to the influence of public opinion; (b) "The children of the poor, the ignorant and the negligent." These can be reached by a vigorous and healthy public opinion; (c) "Apprentices and clerks," who are hurried into offices and workshops from haste of parents or from necessity and (d) colored children.[18]

Educational progress in Connecticut was extremely slow. As late as 1855 in an official report the state superintendent of common schools declared that "a vast number of children among us are growing up without that intellectual and moral culture necessary to make them industrious, respectable, law-abiding citizens."[19] So while Massachusetts, with a comparatively insignificant school fund pressed steadily forward, Connecticut "marked time." Two reasons may be given for the marked diver-

[16] *Ibid.*, 5:123.
[17] *Conn. Com. School Journ.*, (1838), 1:166.
[18] *Ibid.*, 1:165.
[19] Quoted, *Report of Commissioner of Education,* (1897–98), 1:393.

gence, during our period, in the school systems of these two New England states, which, up to 1800, were practically a unit as to educational policy and progress. (1) The smaller percentage of urban and wage-earning population in Connecticut; (2) the weakening of the habit of paying local taxes for educational purposes in Connecticut, on account of the large school fund derived from the sale of public lands.

RHODE ISLAND

In this unique little New England state, no union had ever existed between church and state, and therefore the maintenance of the common school had not been considered to be a true function of the state. Rhode Island had almost completely broken away from the New England ideals. Accordingly, before the opening of our era, to compel a citizen of that commonwealth "to educate his children would have been an invasion of his rights as a free-born Rhode Islander, which would not be endured." In Rhode Island there was no precedent for taxation for educational purposes; no "cheerful habit" of tax-paying for this important purpose had ever been formed. This fact, together with the early peculiar economic and social conditions in the colony, necessarily shaped the course of its educational development quite differently from that of other New England states. The force of public sentiment was distinctly unfavorable to tax-supported public schools.

Attention was previously called to the struggle, culminating in the Dorr war, which led to the extension of the suffrage; and to the rapid development of the public school system thereafter. A factor in this sudden change of sentiment as to public schools, which was not then alluded to, seems to have been due to a reaction among the conservative and propertied classes. Quite likely a picture of the French Revolution arose before their eyes. "The cost of the conflict [Dorr War] taught the most parsimonious, that it was cheaper in a pecuniary respect to prevent than to defray the expenses incident to an uninstructed populace. . . . Under these circumstances, the attention of many of the influential citizens was directed to the situation of the common schools, and the impression seems to have been general and deeply fixed, that no one interest was half so vital as this to the prosperity of the commonwealth, and perhaps even to the security of the new government."[20] In other words extra-legal or unconstitutional acts—the show of force—on the part of the masses of the people caused the conservative interests to demand public schools, to unite with the wage-earners and non-tax-payers on this proposition. "When, therefore they were rejoicing in their escape from the recent convulsion, and looking forward with that wise forecast which its fresh-remembered terror might well inspire, it is not surprising that all the active spirits of the time from the oldest to the youngest, should have deemed this enterprise an object worthy of their attention, and should have entered upon the work with characteristic energy. The manufacturers might well tremble in the presence of the large masses of uninstructed population which were growing around them, and see it written everywhere with a distinctness which none could comprehend so well as they that it was only by educating this population that their business would prosper and their lives and property be secure."[21]

[20] *North American Review* (1848), 67:247–48.
[21] *Ibid.*, 254.

The story which this state unfolds is certainly suggestive. Rhode Island by tradition and habit was averse to tax-supported schools. Suddenly she developed from a predominately commercial and agricultural state to a preeminently manufacturing state. The sharpest and most bitterly contested struggle for the extension of the suffrage which is found in American history, took place in this little state; and within a decade after its conclusion the tax-supported school became a generally accepted institution. In 1848, the rate bill was abolished; but not until nearly a score of years later did it disappear in New York and Connecticut.

NEW YORK

Passing from New England, many factors in our problem are greatly modified. The Puritan régime never obtained a firm foothold outside of New England, although its influence was potent. New York is a state much larger than any one of the three New England states just considered. City and rural districts are widely separated; and her population was, even during this period, cosmopolitan. Wide differences of religious belief existed side by side. The past does not play as important a role as in New England; social conditions are more mobile. In 1812 a law was enacted granting state aid to the public schools of the state. In order to receive the appropriation, each county was required to raise by a tax an amount equal to that appropriated by the state. The office of state superintendent of schools was also created. From time to time the provisions of this law were modified. Later the counties were required to raise an amount by a tax equal to the amount apportioned to them from the state funds; and the local school districts were authorized to levy a tax for building and maintenance of school buildings, supplies, fuel, etc. The remaining amount necessary for compensation of teachers and other expenses was raised by a rate bill. Each person paid according to the number of children he had in school, indigent persons excepted.[22] This was in brief the basis of legislation prior to the Free School Act of 1849. The schools of the city of New York were not included in the state system until 1842, when the first board of education was established.

"During this period [1813–1837], while the common schools of New England, including Massachusetts and Connecticut, were under a partial eclipse, the common school was largely introduced and fostered by New England influence in the state of New York, and gradually improved and became more deserving the confidence of the people."[23] The following table[24] clearly presents to the eye, this steady development.

Dates	No. of school districts reporting	Children taught therein
1816	2,755	140,106
1820	5,763	271,877
1824	7,382	377,034
1826	7,773	425,350
1830	8,609	480,959
1833	9,600	494,959
1840	....	570,000
1845	....	(est) 700,000

22 *Statutes of the State of New York relating to the Common Schools.* (Issued by the Supt. of Common Schools, Albany, 1847.)

23 Mayo, *Rep't of Com. of Education,* (1897–98), 1:437.

24 Compiled from abstract of a rep't of the supt. of common schools of N. Y., given in *Easton, Md. Star,* June 27, 1826; and from Randall, *Common School System of the State of New York,* (1851).

The following table[25] shows the importance of rate-bills in maintaining the public school system of this state.

Dates	Total salary of all teachers of state	Amt. raised by rate bill
1831	$ 586,520.00	$346,807.00
1844	....	509,376.97
1845	992,222.00	447,566.00
1847	1,058,814.64	462,840.44

This is the key to an understanding of the bitterness of the struggle of 1849–1850.

Although the school system was being gradually extended and improved, it was very imperfect and inadequate. "The extension of the free schools in the state is progressing moderately; and laws are passed at nearly every session of the legislature, providing for their establishment in populous and wealthy villages; while the poorer and less populous districts, in the same towns are left to struggle, from year to year, in the best way they can . . . sustaining a school perhaps only four months in the year to secure the next appointment of the public moneys."[26] The apathy and indifference of certain districts of the state were remarkable and discouraging. In 1841, it was ordered that one copy of a *Common School Journal* be sent to every school district in the state of New York. "It is mortifying and painful to state what the truth of history requires us to record, that it is within our personal knowledge that the trustees of many school districts refused to take from the post-office this excellent journal, . . . because they were unwilling to pay from the common funds of their respective

[25] Randall, 31, 36, 47 and 58.

[26] *Rep't of Sup't of Common Schools,* (1847). Quoted Randall, 67.

districts the sum of one shilling a year for postage."[27] As late as 1850, Superintendent Randall made the following appeal: "100,000 destitute children of penury and affliction are silently appealing to you [citizens of New York] for permission to enter the public common schools of your state, and to participate equally with their more fortunate brethren and sisters in the blessings of education."[28]

The peculiar educational situation in New York City must not be overlooked in our study of the development of education in the Empire State. All preceding educational systems were destroyed by the military government of the Revolutionary period. Soon after the termination of the war and the evacuation of the city by the British troops, schools were established by different religious denominations.[29] The non-sectarian Public School Society, which was mentioned in a preceding chapter, had for its object the establishment of "a free school in the city of New York for the education of such poor children as do not belong to, or are not provided for, by any religious society."[30] In 1813, the New York legislature passed a special act providing for a distribution of public money, derived from the state school fund and from local taxation, among the church societies and other schools in the city of New York; but in 1824, another act was passed giving the common council of the city the right to designate the "institutions and schools" which should receive the public money.[31] Soon after the passage of this act the

[27] Quoted, Lossing's *Empire State,* 495, foot note; from Hammond, *Political History of N. Y.,* 3:225.

[28] *New York Tribune,* October 26, 1850.

[29] Palmer, *The New York Public School,* (1905), 11 *et seq.*

[30] Charter of the Society, Draper, *The N. Y. Common School System,* 46; David Hosack, *Memoirs of De Witt Clinton,* 169–173.

[31] Bourne, *History of the Public School Society,* (1870), 404–6.

religious societies were excluded from receiving a share of the public money; but they continued from time to time to demand a portion of these funds for the support of their schools.

After the matter of funds was decided in their favor, the Public School Society began to charge a moderate tuition fee. During the first year (1826) of the experiment the fees amounted to $4,426.00; but in 1831 the receipts from this source were only $1,366.24.[32] In February, 1829, the Society issued a long address to the public regarding the condition of education in the city. It was estimated that there were 24,200 children between the ages of five and fifteen years, living in New York City, who were not attending school. The number attending public schools was declared to be approximately 10,000; and the number attending private schools, 17,500. The ratio of scholars in schools to the total population was estimated to be one to seven. An earnest appeal was made for an increase in taxation so that the pay system might be abolished, and the efficiency of the system improved. "It is obvious from what we have already said," reads the address, "that these schools should be supported from public revenue, should be public property, and should be open to all, not as a charity, but as a matter of common right."[33] A petition was widely circulated, and the aid of the common council obtained. The legislature was urged by the petitioners and the council to levy a tax of one-half of a mill upon the dollar on all property in the city. The legislature, however, only granted a tax levy of one-eighth of one mill. In 1831, an additional tax levy was authorized. As a result, in February, 1832, the schools of the Society were made ab-

[32] Palmer, 68, 69.
[33] Quoted in full by Bourne, 110–118.

solutely free; action in the matter was, however, undoubtedly hastened by the diminution in the amount of the fees, and on account of the dissatisfaction manifested with the fee system. In 1832, steps were taken to establish infant schools.[34] Twelve years later, there were 8,970 pupils enrolled in these schools. In the winter of 1833–1834, evening schools for apprentices were first instituted.[35]

At the time when the workingmen's agitation was at its height, the Public School Society was receiving additional funds, and was improving and extending its system. Yet, strange as it may appear, bearing in mind the extraordinary amount of enthusiasm as to education, the attendance upon the schools of the Society was actually less in 1832 than in 1829. In 1833 and 1834, the effect of the opening of infant schools is very apparent.[36] An his-

[34] These schools were for children from two to six years of age.

[35] Bourne, 157–59.

[36] The attendance upon the schools of the Society was, in 1829, 6,150; in 1830, 6,178; in 1831, 6,323; in 1832, 6,109; in 1833, 7,826; in 1834, 12,537; in 1835, 17,318. Bourne, 32. In addition to the direct effect of the infant schools upon the increase in school attendance three other influences are worthy of notice. (1) Many older children had been kept out of school to care for the younger children. See for example, the report of a joint committee appointed by the workingmen of Philadelphia, (1829); *Delaware Free Press,* March 13, 20 and 27, 1830. The indirect effect of infant schools, therefore, would tend to increase the number of older children in the schools. (2) In 1834, certain established schools for colored children, with an enrollment of 1,608 pupils, were placed in charge of the Public School Society. (3) In 1833 and 1834, loose party association began to be superceded by organized unions of workingmen. The effect of this change upon the educational situation is somewhat problematical; but union organization always opposes the influx of young workers into industry. In 1834 and 1835 is found some consideration of the question of apprenticeship. The workers evidently began to realize that an abuse of the apprentice system tended to lower wages. The glass cutters of New York, in 1835, tried to limit the number of apprentices to be employed in a shop. *The Man,* June 17, 1835. See also *ibid.,* July 25, 1834; *Turn out of the Sailors.* In order that the enthusiasm of the workingmen for education may result in a tangi-

torian of New York City, writing in 1853, of the period 1829 to 1836 approximately, states: "The energy and perseverance exhibited by the Public School Society secured for itself a large share of the public confidence and at the same time gave rise to increased interest in the cause of popular education. Almost the whole of the Common School Fund for the city was intrusted to the disposition of that society. . . . New schools were established. . . . Primary schools . . . were regarded by the public with much favor; and so rapidly were they multiplied that they soon outnumbered those for more advanced pupils."[37]

But opposition to the Society soon began to make itself manifest. If we may judge from the following open letter to the trustees, opposition was, in 1835, quite general in all parts of the city. The writer expresses great dissatisfaction regarding the work of the schools under the direction of the Society. "But there are thousands of people in this city who would acknowledge themselves under infinite obligation to you if you would pocket the money, shut up the schools, and announce to the public your incompetence, your unfitness, and your utter inability to go through with the work you have undertaken."[38] Finally a bitter struggle was precipitated by the Roman Catholics who were growing in strength because of the increasing numbers of immigrants flocking into the city.

The Catholics declared that the funds to be devoted to education should be taken out of the hands of the Pub-

---

ble increase in school attendance, organization and legal enactments seem essential. Otherwise, in individual cases, the desire for increased income from the labor of children overbalances other motives which are more desirable from a social point of view.

[37] Curry, Daniel, *Metropolitan City of America,* 266.

[38] Letter signed by A. M. Printed in *The Man,* January 16, 1835.

lic School Society, and be "placed in the hands of Commissioners elected by the People, who will be accountable to the People for their acts, and who will be sworn not to allow sectarianism to influence the appropriation or distribution of these funds, the selection of books for the use of schools under their control, or of teachers in those schools."[39] It was held that the Society was "a monopoly of an odious character, wholly irresponsible to the people whose agent it professes to be."[40] Finally, Governor Seward, in his message of January, 1842, advocated the establishment of a common school system in the city of New York. He estimated that 20,000 children in that city were not attending school.[41] As a result, the legislature, in 1842, enacted a law providing for a public school system in that city.[42] *The New York Tribune* called this bill an act "to extend the blessings of Sectarian and Political strife into the management of our city Common Schools." The editor declared that Tammany was forced to support this bill because of fear of a defection of two thousand Catholic voters.[43]

After the enactment of this law the schools under the control of the Public School Society steadily declined. In 1852, the Society terminated its existence, and turned over the schools in its charge to the board of education. The Public School Society had, in 1842, undoubtedly passed its period of greatest usefulness; its methods and management did not harmonize with ideals of the time.

[39] Letter signed "Catholics." *N. Y. Tribune,* November 24, 1841.

[40] Resolutions adopted at a mass meeting of "Catholics and others favorable to an alteration in the present Public School System." *N. Y. Tribune,* November 19, 1841.

[41] *N. Y. Tribune,* January 5, 1842. Also H. J. Desmond, *The Know-Nothing Party,* 28–33.

[42] The vote was, in the Senate, 13 for and 12 against; in House, 80 to 20 respectively.

[43] *N. Y. Tribune,* April 11, 1842.

The results of this sectarian conflict were productive of good. "The importance of the controversy that sprang up around this corporation in the city of New York can hardly be overrated. . . . Indeed, the reorganization of the New York City schools assured the great popular majority of votes in that city in favor of an absolute free school system for the State, which carried the point."[44]

Passing from the city to the state, we need only call attention to the law of 1849 which did away with the odious rate-bill throughout the entire state. It reads; "Common schools in the several school districts in this State shall be free to all persons residing in the district over five and under twenty-one years of age."[45] The schools were to be supported by the distribution of state funds and by local taxation. The fight of 1849 and 1850 was merely one to prevent the lopping off of the rate-bill. Since 1812, local taxation had been utilized for the public schools; but it was the increase in this tax which stirred up such bitter opposition.

Massachusetts and Connecticut, with a comparatively homogeneous population, and still nursing a fear of any sort of centralized administration, delayed the adoption of any systematic plan of school supervision until the latter part of the decade of the thirties. Rapidly increasing heterogeneity of population made possible and desirable, the work of Horace Mann and Henry Barnard. In New York, on the contrary, the first act looking toward state supervision was enacted as early as 1812, with apparently little opposition; and today the school administration of the state of New York is perhaps centralized to a greater extent than in any other state in the

[44] Mayo, *Rep't of Commissioner of Education,* 1897–98, 1:452, 454.
[45] *Act to establish free schools throughout the state* in *Statutes of New York, 1849,* sec. 1.

Union. New York has "had supervision by State officers since 1812, by county or district officers from 1841 to 1847 and from 1856 to the present time, and by town officers from 1795 to 1856."[46] This is one of the significant and interesting features of the educational development of the state of New York.

PENNSYLVANIA

In the educational development of Pennsylvania, three points are especially worthy of notice; the prominence given to sectarian schools, the unusual odium which attached to the "pauper" children attending the public schools, and the evident influence of the New England man in the establishment of the free school system. The acts of 1802 and 1809 carried out the provisions of the state constitution, and provided for the free instruction for the children of the poor. These acts with some modifications remained in force until the passage of the free school act of 1834. The law of 1809 "compelled parents to make public records of their poverty—to pauperize themselves, so to speak, by sending their children to school with this invidious mark upon them. Another disagreeable feature of the law was, that it required teachers to make oath or affidavit of all such children too poor to pay for their own schooling, whereupon the County Commissioners were required to compensate the schoolmaster in charge. Under this pauper act, so much odium was attached to those who attended the schools, that many people preferred to keep their children at home in ignorance rather than suffer the humiliation to which they were subjected by those whose parents could afford

[46] Draper, *The N. Y. Common School System*, (1890), 59.

the expense of educating them privately."[47] Thus this pauper clause, inserted probably because of the general prevalence of sectarian schools, tended to discredit the public school system, to accentuate class distinctions, and to increase the influence and numbers of the sectarian and private schools. Those who could afford to pay rate bills sent their children elsewhere and many who could not kept their children out of school entirely. Even a decade after the passage of the free school act, the private schools "were still all-powerful, and those attending them only too frequently looked with disdain upon those compelled through necessity in many instances to attend the 'state schools.'"[48] Pennsylvania became unhappily distinguished for the large number of her children who were not attending school. "By a recent estimate made by competent persons, it appears that there are one million children in the United States, growing up in ignorance, without the means of education; of these 250,000 are said to be in Pennsylvania."[49] Another account states that in 1837, more than 250,000, out of 400,000 children in the state were destitute of school instruction;[50] a third estimate places the number at 200,000 in 1835.[51]

As has already been noticed in the fight of 1834–1835 for the free school law, the influence of the New England men was in favor of the law. "In a group of ten counties found on the northern border of the state, settled largely

[47] Riddle, Wm., *School History of Lancaster, Penn.*, 21.

[48] *Ibid.*, 21.

[49] *Newark Sentinel.* Quoted in *Philadelphia Liberator,* June 29, 1833.

[50] *Portland Transcript.* Quoted in *Farmers' and Mechanics' Journal,* September 8, 1838.

[51] *Pittsburgh Visitor.* Quoted in *Phila. American Daily Advertiser,* January 21, 1835.

from New England and New York, there was not found a single hostile district. It was in this region that the first settlement in the beautiful Wyoming valley by a Connecticut colony had established the New England system of common schools before the Revolutionary war. These counties were not only intensely patriotic, but they also forced the brief acknowledgement of universal education into the constitutions of 1779 and 1790. And here had been found the solid column of support for the gallant leadership of Thaddeus Stevens, which had upheld the new school law during the assault that followed its enactment."[52] The following testimony from a county having a mixed population is also pertinent. "As has been said, there was from the time of the first settlement of this old town the nucleus of an English population. It was small in number at first, but all-powerful in scholastic training and religious conviction, elements that have ever dominated the social, political and intellectual life of this city from then to the present day, (1905). This, however, is in no way intended to convey the impression that the Lutheran, the Moravian and German Reformed Congregations, the oldest with the possible exception of the Friends, were any less intelligent or aggressive. But they differ from the English settlers in adhering more strictly to their own denominational schools and places of worship; and they manifested little interest, at least for many years in the political and secular affairs of the community."[53] Every county in the northern tier of counties was overwhelmingly in favor of living up to the conditions imposed by the free school law; and five out of seven on the western row were favorable to it. Among the counties most strongly against it and in which nearly

[52] Mayo, *Rep't of the Com. of Education,* 1897–98, 474.
[53] Riddle, *School History of Lancaster,* (1905), 7–8.

all districts rejected the provisions of the law, were Berks, Dauplin [*sic*], Lebanon, Lehigh, and Union.[54] As late as 1866, twenty-three districts in eleven different counties, having at least six thousand children of school age, still refused to put the public schools in operation, and rejected the grant of state aid.[55] Governor Wolf in his message of December, 1835, said: "The state exclusive of the city and county of Philadelphia, which are not embraced within the provisions of the law [1834 and the supplemental act of 1835], and the counties of Greene, Columbia, Montgomery and Clearfield, from which no reports have been received has been divided into 907 school districts, of this number 536 have accepted and 371 rejected the provisions of the law."[56] When we remember that, if a district rejected the provisions of the law, it lost all claim to state aid in educating its children, we are able to picture the bitterness of the opposition to the free schools.

Like New York City, Philadelphia, the largest city of the state was favored by a special school law. In 1818, a special law was passed to establish a better and less expensive system of schools in the city, than those in operation under the general state law of 1809. However, these schools were in principle "pauper schools" exactly as were those organized under the state law; "and they are more to be commended only because they were organized into a system under the management of responsible officers, and provision was made for the building of schoolhouses, the preparation of teachers and the furnishing of text-books."[57] However, these schools gradually became "so much like free schools that the transition of

[54] Wickersham, (1886), 322.
[55] *Ibid.*, 562.
[56] Quoted in *Hazard's Register of Pennsylvania*, (1836), 16:372.
[57] Wickersham, (1886), 286–87.

1836 was scarcely felt except in the multitudes of new pupils who applied for admission."[58] As stated above, the law of 1834 did not apply to Philadelphia. The special law of 1836, amended the act of 1818 so as to admit all children. The power of conservative and sectarian interests is particularly noticeable in this city. "The city of Philadelphia and the four adjacent counties were largely, in their influential classes, still dominated by the religious sect of the Friends or Quakers. This body, from the first, had been strongly attached to a special parochial system of education, and had built up, not only for the higher, but largely for the poorer classes, including the neglected colored people, an educational system satisfactory to itself. In this, still the most influential, wealthy, and cultivated section of the state, after a three-years experiment, little more than one-half of the districts in these counties had accepted the common schools. To meet this condition the law had been modified in the interest of the prevailing system to subsidize all schools willing to come under a merely nominal control of the state, retaining the power of appointing their own teachers."[59]

In both cities, New York and Philadelphia, where the peculiar evils of modern urban life were early apparent, the need of education for the children of the working classes was felt, before it was discerned elsewhere in the two states. To meet this demand sectarian and private schools became numerous; and although these cities contained a large wage-earning and non- or small tax-paying population, such was the influence of the private and sectarian schools that the development of the public school system in these two cities actually lagged behind,

[58] *Ibid.*, 287.

[59] Mayo, *Rep't of Com. of Education,* (1897–98), 474.

in certain respects, that of the general system in their respective states. While at the time of their inception these non-public schools represented progress; in the course of events, they became conservative and blocked the way leading toward a public school system, uniform with the remainder of the state. They were animated by a conception of educational methods and duties which was incompatible with modern industrial and urban conditions; their ideals were chiefly traditional and undemocratic.

Contrasting the educational development in these two important states, it seems that the earlier enactment of a free school law in Pennsylvania was due in no small measure, to the peculiar odium which attached itself to the "pauper clause" in the early school law of that state. This in turn was due to the strength of the German and sectarian influence. The milder form of the early school law in New York actually delayed the final enactment of a free school law, devoid of the pauper stigma. The Pennsylvania struggle was one in which nationalities and religious sects played a considerable rôle. The New York climax came a decade and one-half later, when the contrast between urban and rural, and between wage-earners and large tax-payers was much more definitely marked. In New York and Rhode Island the student may see most clearly the forces which have hastened the evolution of the tax-supported public school system.

Before passing on, attention should be called to a notable report on education prepared by a committee appointed, in September, 1829, by the workingmen of Philadelphia.[60] The committee, which reported about

[60] Report printed in full. *Delaware Free Press,* March 13, 20 and 27, 1830. *Free Enquirer,* March 6 and 13, 1830. *Working Man's Advocate,* March 6, 1830.

five months later, painted a very dismal picture of educational conditions in Pennsylvania. With the exception of Philadelphia, Lancaster and Pittsburg, which were favored by special school laws, it was found that the schools of the state were in a deplorable condition. The provisions of the act of 1809 were frequently inoperative. "The funds appropriated by the act have, in some instances, been embezzled by fraudulent agents; and in others, partial returns of the children have been made, and some have been illegally and intentionally excluded from participating in the provisions of the law."

This committee then presented its proposals for remedying the deficiencies in the then-existing public school system. Remembering that this report was written three-quarters of a century ago, it is certainly not an exaggeration to designate it as a remarkable document. First and foremost is the demand that the "pauper clause" in the school law be removed, and the schools opened free to all. Then four important proposals were made which are worthy of particular notice. (1) Schools for the care and instruction of infants were favored. It was asserted that the young children of the poor could not be properly taken care of at home. (2) It was recommended that at least one manual labor school be established in each county. These schools, it was urged, would reduce the expense to the community by enabling the children to maintain themselves; and would make it possible for the poor to send their older children to school. It was pointed out that "the practice, formerly universal, of schooling apprentices, has, of late years, greatly diminished, and is still diminishing;" manual labor schools would tend to remedy this evil. (3) The committee favored a system of school management similar to that now employed in "school cities" or in the George Junior Republic. (4) It bewailed the prevalence of the vice of intemperance among the city youth; and emphasized the importance of, and necessity for a plan of education which would combine study, play and manual labor. Such a plan "by its almost entire occupation of the time of the pupils either in labor, study or recreation, by the superior facilities it affords for engrossing their whole attention and by its capability of embracing the whole juvenile population furnishes, we believe, the only rational hope of ultimately averting the ruin which is threatened by this extensive vice." This sentiment clearly anticipates many of the most modern ideas as to the treatment of juvenile delinquents. The parental school is now doing the kind of work this committee recommended. The men who framed this report evidently did not, however, anticipate immediate important, practical results. "It is to be expected," reads the report, "that political demagogism, professional monopoly and monied influence, will conspire as hitherto (with solitary exceptions more or less numerous) they ever have conspired against everything that has promised to be an equal benefit to the whole population."

VERMONT

The progress of educational evolution in this New England state is instructive because Vermont is a typical New England commonwealth. Her people possessed all the traditions, customs and habits of the early New Englanders. But Vermont, unlike Massachusetts, Connecticut and Rhode Island, has remained, down to the present era, a preponderantly rural state. No large cities are found in the state. The direct influence of the growth of an industrial population and of cities is very small; indirectly, of course, the influence of educational advance in other states has been felt. The first settlers of Vermont came chiefly from the colonies of Massachusetts and Connecticut,[61] and were animated by the same religious spirit. That the people of Vermont possessed all the peculiar qualities of the typical New England Yankee as to personal independence, is clearly shown by the first report of the board of school commissioners in 1828. "No system of common school education can be of lasting or essential benefit to the state unless it receives the cordial cooperation and support of parents and instructors. But so generally diffused through the great mass of the community is the sense of personal as well as political independence, and so sleepless is the jealousy of arbitrary power, which is almost instinctive in the popular mind, that the attempt, however well-intentioned, to dictate the books to be used in our common schools is regarded by many as invasion of the right of private judgment, and consequently as incompatible with the genius of our free institutions."[62]

In 1856, nearly twenty years later than in Massachusetts, "a rising wave of a popular educational revival lifted the fathers of the State to the establishment of a board of education," similar to that of Massachusetts.[63] The educational uplift which Massachusetts, Connecticut and Rhode Island experienced in the thirties and forties seems to have reached Vermont ten to twenty years later. For example one of Vermont's historians writing in 1853, declared: "But while Vermont is not perhaps behind any of her sister states in the general intelligence of the people, we cannot help thinking that the general interests of education have, for several years

[61] Smith and Rann, *History of Rutland County,* 201.
[62] Quoted in *Rep't of Com. of Education,* (1897–98), 1:408.
[63] *Ibid.,* 413.

past, been culpably neglected. While other states have been rapidly improving their schools and school systems, Vermont has remained nearly stationary."[64] Even in 1867, the state superintendent of education declared that the condition of the schools for a score of years was a "source of grief and mortification to a large majority of our citizens."[65] In 1856, the then superintendent asserted that "the public mind seemed to have sunk into a state of torpor and indifference, the legitimate and usual consequences of State inaction."[66]

The inherited New England belief in the value of universal education, and the reflected influence of progress in neighboring states, kept alive the educational spark in Vermont. The lesson is that homogeneity of population, absence of wide differences of interests among the inhabitants, and the predominance of the middle classes did not give birth to the modern tax-supported public school system; if these were the potent influences, Vermont should have stood in the forefront of educational development during our period. The story of Vermont points toward the conclusion, certainly, that the tax-supported school system evolved out of heterogeneity of population, improvement in methods of production, the specialization of industry, the division of labor, the growth of factories and the separation of home life from industrial occupations.

OHIO

Turning to the West, where frontier influences were still predominant, let us examine into the causes of the trend

64 Thompson, Zadock, *History of Vermont,* (1853), pt. 2, 142.
65 Rann, W. S., *History of Chittenden County,* 211.
66 *Rep't Com. of Education,* (1897–98), 1:414.

of educational development in this section. The first act which made any attempt to carry out the constitutional requirements as to education in the state of Ohio, was passed in January, 1821. This act permitted the funds derived from the sale of the school lands to be applied to the erection of schoolhouses. Each district might determine for itself the amount of taxation to be applied to school purposes. Rate bills were to be levied.[67] The next step in educational development in Ohio was taken one year later by the appointment of a commission to report on a common-school system. This measure was passed after resort to "log-rolling;" a combination was formed between the friends of education and of canals.[68] The law of 1825 was the result of the labors of this committee. This law furnished the real foundation of the school system of the state. It was made the duty of the township trustees to organize school-districts. A county school tax of one-half mill was ordered and provisions were made for distributing the funds derived from the school lands among the school districts. Examination of teachers was mandatory, and the required branches to be taught were prescribed to be the famous three R's.[69] "The school law of 1825 was not well received in even a majority of the principal towns of the state, and eleven years elapsed before adequate steps were taken to render the system it provided for efficient."[70]

"Almost coincident with the eastern educational revival under Horace Mann in 1837, a popular wave of public school enthusiasm struck Ohio."[71] The keynote of

[67] King, Rufus, *Ohio*, 348; *Barnard's Journal of Education*, (1859), 6:82 *et seq*. Dexter, *History of Education in the U. S.*, 105.

[68] King, Rufus, *Ohio*, 348.

[69] Hinsdale, *Rep't of Com. of Education*, (1901), 1:134.

[70] *Barnard's Journal of Education*, (1859), 6:85.

[71] Dexter, 105.

the act of 1837 which resulted from this "popular wave" was supervision, as was true of the act passed in Massachusetts. Samuel Lewis was appointed state superintendent of schools soon after the passage of this act.[72] Many acts were passed between 1825 and 1850 changing the rate of taxation for school purposes.[73] In 1853, the rate-bill was finally relegated to the past. The curriculum of the common schools of Ohio was extremely narrow during the period under discussion. Grammar and geography were first ordered to be placed in the curriculum in 1848.[74] As late as 1845, many school directors of the districts, "forbade the teaching of any branches except reading, writing and arithmetic."[75]

The course of educational advance in Ohio during this period was unmarked by spectacular episodes. Two points, however, must not be overlooked in the consideration of the educational history of Ohio. (1) Broad suffrage provisions are found in the first constitution of the state. (2) Agricultural interests were perdominate [*sic*] in the state; there was no marked opposition between rural and urban populations previous to 1850. The constitutional provisions and the early laws as to education seem to have been attained through the efforts of men imbued with New England ideals. One reason for this opinion rests on the prevalence of the New England district system, and the extreme decentralization of the school administration. Until very recently the school districts were practically free from all effective supervision. Another

[72] This office was established in 1840. From 1840 to 1853 the secretary of state acted as superintendent of schools. For analysis of the school history of Ohio, see Orth, S. P., *The centralization of administration in Ohio* in *Columbia Studies,* 16: No. 3, 73.

[73] *Barnard's Journal,* (1859), 6:545–46.

[74] *Ibid.,* 95.

[75] *Ibid.,* 90.

support for this opinion is found in the refusal on the part of many towns to accept the provisions of the act of 1825.[76]

The New England man seems to have been an important factor in the political history of Ohio. "A majority of the legislators of our State were, a few years before the establishment of our school system, natives, or descendants from natives, of New England, and, in due time, they gave efficient aid to the enactment of the school law. In the middle and southern portions of our State, most of the first settlers were from Pennsylvania, and from states further south."[77] "In the Ohio legislature in 1822 there were thirty-eight of middle state birth, thirty-three of southern (including Kentucky), and twenty-five of New England."[78] The Western Reserve, consisting of a block of twelve counties in the northeastern portion of the state, and peopled largely from Connecticut, fostered education from the outset, and was no small factor in determining the course of educational development.[79]

"The early immigrants to Ohio from New England considered schools and churches as among their first wants . . . those from Pennsylvania considered them the last . . . while those from New Jersey, and the few from Maryland, Virginia, the other Southern states, had their views of education fixed upon so high a scale that nothing less than colleges, or seminaries of the highest class could claim much of their attention, or seem to require any extraordinary efforts for their establishment."[80] Professor Turner speaking of certain conditions in the dec-

[76] See previous citation *Barnard's Journal,* 6:85.

[77] Foote, J. P., *The Schools of Cincinnati,* (1855), 35.

[78] Turner, F. J., *Colonization of the West* in *Amer. Hist. Rev.,* 2: 308. Also *Niles' Register,* 21:368.

[79] Mathews, A., *Ohio and her Western Reserve,* 196.

[80] Foote, *Schools of Cincinnati,* (1855), 35.

ade, 1820–1830, writes: "The West was too new a section to have developed educational facilities to any large extent. The pioneers' poverty, as well as the traditions of the southern interior from which they so largely came discouraged extensive expenditures for public schools."[81]

The principle of public support of common schools seems to have been accepted in theory at least by an influential fraction of the population of the commonwealth at the time of the adoption of the first state constitution. In Massachusetts, as has been stated, the educational advance during the period was toward better supervision of the schools. This movement was more successful in that state than in her sister state, Connecticut, where industry was not so important a factor in the state's economic life as in Massachusetts. In Ohio, a state which inherited, in no small degree, the New England traditions and ideals, but lagged behind both Massachusetts and Connecticut in industrial and urban development, supervision failed of practical results comparable with those of Massachusetts. Demand for the centralization of educational authority, in the United States, tends to become strong where the population consists of widely divergent social and industrial factors; and when industrial and urban population are important factors in the community.

THE SOUTH

The failure of the common school system in the South previous to the Civil war is important, in view of the fact that our study of the North has forced upon us the conclusion that the cities and the working classes were

[81] Turner, *Colonization of the West* in *Amer. Hist. Rev.*, 2:326.

chiefly instrumental in placing our schools upon a tax-supported basis. A contemporary writer has so well summarized the forces which operated in the South during our period that it is advisable to quote a paragraph. Before the Civil war, "the towns and cities assumed comparatively slight importance. The South had little export trade of manufactured articles. Its cotton went to England and New England cotton mills. It had not reached the point of working up its raw products for commercial purposes. Hence, as a distinctly manufacturing center, the city was quite unknown, and with the majority of the population engaged in agriculture the town exerted no dominant influence. The sentiments that characterized the rural population permeated the towns and formed public opinion in the South."[82] To this must be added the entire lack of New England traditions, the presence of a slave population, and the prevalence of the plantation system. These influences seem sufficient to account for the trend of educational development in this section.

In recent years industries are springing up in many of the southern states; and the problems relating to education and to child labor are becoming acute. This section of the nation is passing through a period of development similar to that through which New England and New York passed nearly three-fourths of a century earlier.[83] The following poster was used in a campaign of education in Georgia in 1905.[84] "Vote for your children. Local taxation for education is the cheapest insurance for the coming generation. It's right! It pays! Vote out Igno-

[82] Simons, May W., *American Journal of Sociology*, 10:383.

[83] The writer, *The South during the Last Decade* in *Sewanee Review*, April, 1904.

[84] Now in the hands of Prof. R. T. Ely.

rance. Vote in the only Basis of Economic Progress." Here is a recrudescence of the economic argument in the form in which it was used in the North more than half a century ago. The educational phenomena of the South strikingly strengthen the opinion that modern educational progress and industrial evolution proceed hand in hand.[85]

The experience of the Carolinas throws some light upon the problem before us. In 1811, South Carolina passed a free school law. This law did not provide for local taxation, but authorized a state appropriation of three hundred dollars each to as many schools as there were representatives in the lower house of the state legislature. Every citizen was entitled, according to the law, to send his children to the free schools; but in case more children applied than could be conveniently accommodated, the children of the poor were to be given the preference.[86] In December, 1814, an attempt was made to repeal this law. "The act which established a fund for the support of Free Schools through the state of South Carolina has been repealed! And this too, notwithstanding a committee of the Legislature unanimously reported that they had examined the reports of the Commissioners of 23 school districts and found that no less than 4,651 children had been educated the last year from the fund; and that the act had been productive of unbounded good and no evil. To the honor of the Charleston representation it ought to be stated that they all voted against the

[85] A southern commercial convention, held in Memphis in 1853, recommended to the people of the South, "the education of their youth at home, as far as practicable." *DeBow's Review,* 15:268.

[86] Cooper, Thomas, *Statutes at large of South Carolina,* (1839), 5: 639–41. Also Courtenay, Mayor William A., *Education in South Carolina,* (1886); a pamphlet issued by the city council of Charleston.

repeal."[87] The Senate refused to concur with the House;[88] and the law remained upon the statute books during the entire period, 1820 to 1850.[89] Its provisions were not well carried out;[90] as its execution was left to districts and was without centralized control. In 1853, it was written: "We have the whole work to begin anew."[91]

A public school system was inaugurated in North Carolina in 1840. In 1858, it was stated that "upon a calm review of the entire facts, it is neither immodest nor unjust to assert that North Carolina is clearly ahead of all the slave-holding states with her system of public instruction, while she compares favorably in several respects with some of the New England and Northwestern States."[92] Economic and social conditions in North Carolina approximated those of Vermont or Ohio much more closely than did the conditions existing in the other states of the slave-owning South;[93] and here is found the closest approach to the rural school system of the North. In South Carolina, the significant feature is the influence exerted by the city of Charleston in favor of free public schools.

[87] *Columbia Centinel* (Boston), January 4, 1815, 2.

[88] *Boston Gazette,* January 12, 1815, 2.

[89] In 1826, there were four free schools established in Charleston. Mills, Robert, *Statistics of Charleston,* (1826), 438. The total population of the city in 1820, including slaves, was 24,870.

[90] Message of Gov. Andrew Pickens, *National Intelligencer,* December 9, 1817.

[91] Thornwell, J. H., *Letter to His Excellency Gov. Manning on Public Instruction in South Carolina,* (1853), 28.

[92] Rev. C. H. Wiley, Sup't of Common Schools of N. C., *N. C. Journal of Education,* February, 1858. Quoted by Smith, Chas. L., *History of Education in North Carolina.* Issued by Com. of Education, (1888), 169.

[93] Bruce, P. A., *The Rise of the New South* in *History of North America,* 17.

DELAWARE

The state of Delaware furnishes some very interesting and instructive material. This state is quite narrow in comparison with its length; and is composed of three counties only,—New Castle on the north, Kent in the middle, and Sussex on the south. The only important city is Wilmington, situated in New Castle county. In 1850, one-third of the population of this county were included within the corporate limits of Wilmington. Sussex county was a purely agricultural county; in 1850 nearly seven per cent. of its population were slaves. Kent county, containing the village of Dover, was of a distinctly rural character, but only about one and one-half per cent. of its population were slaves.

1840[94]	Population	Number of persons employed in agriculture	Number of persons employed in manufacture	Number of primary and common schools
New Castle Co. .	33,120	5,119	2,805	60
Kent Co.	19,872	4,604	659	46
Sussex Co.	25,093	6,292	596	46

1850[95]	Population	Slave population	Public Schools		
			Taxation for	Pupils	Tax per pupil
New Castle Co.	42,780	394	$8,975	3,227	$2.78
Kent Co.	22,816	347	4,161	2,403	1.77
Sussex Co.	25,936	1,549	1,286	3,340	0.38

	Population
Dover (village), Kent Co.	3,790
New Castle (village), New Castle Co.	2,737
Wilmington (village), New Castle Co.	8,367

94 *Census Reports* (1840).
95 *Ibid.* (1850).

In 1829, a local option school law, fathered by a New England man, Willard Hall,[96] was passed by the state legislature. The principles underlying this law, as afterwards stated by Mr. Hall, represented a cross between the southern and the New England idea as to the educational functions of the state. "The Report of the Massachusetts Board of Education declares that the cardinal principle which lies at the foundation of their educational system is, that all the children of the State, shall be educated by the State. Let it be distinctly remarked that this is not the principle of our school system; but that our school system is founded upon the position that the people must educate their own children and that all the State should do, or can do for any useful effect, is to organize them into communities so as to act together for that purpose and help and encourage them to act efficiently."[97] This is the voice of the liberal, not of the democrat.

This school law operated fairly well in New Castle county: but not so well in Kent and Sussex.[98] In New Castle county, in 1852, the amount raised by tax was double that of 1832. In Kent and Sussex counties, it had only increased about one-fifth, and was actually less than in 1841.[99] In 1850, one-third of the total population of New Castle county lived in Wilmington; and the amount of money per pupil, raised by taxation was $2.78. But the strictly rural county of Sussex, with a

[96] Willard Hall (1780–1875), was born in Massachusetts, and graduated from Harvard in 1799. He was a lawyer and a politician, and became the first superintendent of public schools of Delaware.

[97] Speech before a state school convention, at Dover, in 1843. Quoted *Barnard's Journal of Education,* 16:370.

[98] Willard Hall in a letter to Dr. Barnard. *Barnard's Journal of Education,* 16:129.

[99] Powell, *History of Education in Delaware,* (1893), 144. Issued by Com. of Education.

comparatively large slave population, raised only thirty-eight and a fraction cents per pupil. This striking contrast cannot be adequately explained, as has been argued,[100] by the influence of annual school conventions in New Castle county and the absence of their influence in Sussex county. The dissimilarity between the economic and social conditions was, as the preceding tables have shown, very great; and it is in this circumstance that we must look for a more adequate explanation of the educational phenomena exhibited by these two counties.

In the history of the development of the school system of Delaware from 1820 to 1850, therefore, three points stand out prominently. First, the initiative of the educated leader impelled by humanitarian impulses. Second, the favorable influence of the urban population and of the workingmen. The workingmen of Wilmington and New Castle county, like those of New York and Philadelphia, were insistent, at the opening of the decade of the thirties, in their demands for better educational facilities.[101] Third, the retarding influence of the rural population, particularly where slaves were owned. About 1850, democratic tendencies were beginning to overwhelm the liberal sentiment. "Public sentiment throughout the State was rapidly increasing in favor of removing taxation for the maintenance of schools beyond the caprices, narrowness, and prejudices of the voter."[102] In this movement New Castle county naturally assumed the leadership.

100 Powell, 147. Also *Barnard's Journal of Education,* 16:129.

101 *Delaware Free Press,* January 9, July 31, August 28, September 18 and 25 and October 9, 1830.

102 Powell, 147.

7. Concluding Remarks

What were the immediate influences which produced the educational advance of the period 1820–1850? Which is fundamental, educational progress or industrial and social changes? What answer does our investigation offer? The facts presented in the preceding chapters seem to warrant the conclusion that economic and social conditions are the sources from which spring educational methods and ideals rather than the reverse. It is an old fallacy that institutions and forms of governments mold a people; on the contrary it is much nearer the truth to maintain that political institutions and laws are outward and visible manifestations of the spirit and ideals of a people. Similarly, educational systems while introducing important modifying factors are true products of the industrial and social life of a people. The New England school system did not arise in the South or in Rhode Island during the colonial period, because of different economic and social conditions. Rhode Island, becoming predominately an industrial state, adopted the tax-supported system before 1850; but the South, committed to the plantation system and to the institution of slavery, adhered to the old policy of private schools. Today when industry is quickening her pulses, the demand for efficient tax-supported schools is growing insistent. Manual training and laboratory work were not placed in the curriculum until sub-division of labor and the factory system made such additions imperative. The demand for tax-supported schools became strong and vigorous after the growth of the industrial class and the development of the modern city with its heterogeneous population. The evidence adduced in the preceding chapters shows that the tax-supported, state-maintained public school is essentially an outgrowth of industrial evolution.

Universal education is a modern doctrine; it is borne along on the rising tide of modern democracy. It springs from the same sources as does democracy. Universal education did not fit into the program of the feudal or the military state. The idea of taxation for the support of the common schools and of compulsory attendance upon the same is undoubtedly foreign to the spirit of the eighteenth century as expressed by the English people. The doctrine of natural rights does not harmonize with the demand for free tax-supported schools. The modern system of education is a product of democracy, not of liberalism. The old theocratic idea of the religious necessity of education, transmitted through generations of New England men is an important element of strength which the past bequeathed to the modern movement; but the present can never be explained without a consideration of the past.

Educational aims, methods and ideals are modified as industrial and social conditions change. There are no hard and fast standards of educational values. While no one of the states presents the different forces isolated, as one would desire for a laboratory experiment; such an examination as has been made in the preceding chapters does disclose many important tendencies. A rural community has one standard of education and a city people another; this is exemplified in New York, Pennsylvania, and Rhode Island. The prevalence of domestic industry produces one attitude, and the general adoption of the factory system another attitude upon the subject of education, and the relation of the state to the school system; this is evident if a comparison is made between New England before the War of 1812 and after 1820. In a district where a dominant religious belief is found, a different standard of educational values will probably obtain than where many sects are present. It was the animosity between the religious factions which hastened the adoption of the public school system in New York City. In Pennsylvania the attitude of certain religious sects was quite different, in counties where several sects were mingled, from that which obtained in counties where one of these beliefs was predominant. Colonial New England viewed the educational problem differently before and after the passage of the acts of religious toleration. Again, the question is decided differently in a state possessing a comparatively homogeneous population than in a state where the population is very heterogeneous. In the state of New York is found an extreme differentiation of urban from rural types, and between rich and poor. In this state are found large numbers of raw immigrants of many nationalities. It is peopled by an extremely heterogeneous mass of human beings. And in New York state supervision of the public school system early obtained a foot-hold. Today she is the leader in the work of state supervision of schools.

Three general features which modified the course of educational progress in the North during the period under consideration, ought to be pointed out. (a) There was no dominant religious system. "The absence of a dominant church has helped to protect the school system of the United States from the perils and odium of religious strife."[1] (b) A constant stream of immigration

[1] Adams, Francis, *The Theory of Free Schools,* 6.

flowed into every state, and from the older states a stream of emigration poured out as well. This double stream tended to drain the rural districts of the older states of their best and most progressive blood, and to introduce into the country many foreigners of varying degrees of ability. (c) The control of the schools by small local units.

The altruistic theory of the development of the United States public tax-supported school system seems in the light of the facts to be utterly inadequate to account for the phenomenon. It has been shown that the humanitarian leaders were drawn from a class which was not in sympathy with the industrial conditions of the period; they were members of a class which did not profit, but lost through the industrial transformation which occurred during the first half of the nineteenth century. These men appealed to the past. The peculiar exigencies of the time brought them and the masses of the people into agreement as to certain planks of a platform of principles; but fundamentally, the ideals of these two parties were radically at variance. John Ruskin is a notable example of a distinguished humanitarian leader. Ruskin lived in a mystical golden past; he idealized and glorified a period and a social condition which can never return. This man joined hands with the workingmen, and has been termed a socialist; but, at heart, he was an aristocrat. He abhorred the modern ideals of democracy; the demand for universal suffrage, for example, he considered to be caused by a delusion. The vitality of the movement for tax-supported schools was derived not from the humanitarian leaders, but from the growing class of wage-earners.

If generalization is warranted by the data before us, the conclusion is warranted that, in modern times, the trend of educational advance is determined by economic evolution. On the one hand, the student of educational problems, who is striving to improve the work of the public schools, must study the trend of industrial and social evolution; and, on the other hand, the political economist and social scientist must consider the economic and social significance of uniform advance in educational and industrial evolution.

Appendix I
England and the United States

A COMPARISON

In England, the trend of educational advance was very different during the period 1820 to 1850, from that which has been traced in the United States. There the rise of the factory system and the development of industrial towns antedated the course of industrial progress in this country. All the phenomena relating to the congestion of the laboring population, pauperism, child and women labor, juvenile crime and the like, were to be found in England in an aggravated form; but the free tax-supported school did not obtain a foot-hold on English soil during this period. The industrial conditions which seem to have been such a potent factor in our educational advance, were found in England. If England's industrial progress during this era paralleled, or was a step in advance, of that in the United States, why did not educational advance keep pace? Does England offer a flat contradiction to the view that educational progress is the necessary consequence of industrial advance?

In 1850, a Traveling Bachelor of the University of Cambridge published the results of a careful investigation as to the social condition and the education of the masses of the English people. A very dismal picture is painted.[1] Of all the children living in England and Wales, between the ages of five and fourteen years, it was declared, according to reliable information, over one-half were not attending any school.[2] "In most of our schools, it is necessary in order to provide salaries for the teachers, and funds for the support of the school, to charge from 2d to 4d a week per head for the instruction of scholars. This absolutely excludes the children of all paupers, and of all poor persons."[3] This writer declared that while in England, in 1850, "the aristocracy is richer and more powerful than that of any other country in the world, the poor are more depressed, more pauperized, more numerous in comparison to the other classes, more irreligious, and very much worse educated than the poor of any other European nation, solely excepting Russia, Turkey, South Italy, Portugal and Spain."[4] The above is a deliberate statement of an English scholar, made after a careful investigation; it is not the opinion of an agitator.

During the period which we have been considering there occurred three important agitations in which the working people of England were deeply interested; the movement which bore as its fruit the Reform Bill of 1832, the Chartist movement, and the fight for the repeal of the Corn Laws. Two of the struggles were successful in the main; one failed of direct results. A brief consideration of these important movements may throw light upon our problem, and enable us to more clearly discern the forces which were at work. It is probably indisputable that these agitations were the direct outcome of the

[1] Kay, Joseph, *The Social Condition and Education of the People*, 2:461, *et seq.*

[2] *Ibid.*, 461

[3] *Ibid.*, 464.

[4] *Ibid.*, 538.

development of industry and the rise of a manufacturing and commercial class, and the growth of a wage-earning, urban-dwelling population. In England at the opening of the nineteenth century, political and economic power was almost exclusively in the hands of a land-owning aristocracy,—a social factor of little consequence in the United States. The Reform Bill extended political power to the middle—commercial and manufacturing—class; this legislation was the outcome of a union between the middle and wage-earning classes; but the most valuable and desirable fruits of the victory which was attained by means not strictly legal, to put it mildly, were appropriated, in the main, by the middle class; and only a sop was thrown to their quondam allies, the wage-earners. "The working class in the opinion of many of their ablest and most influential representatives were not merely left out but shouldered out. This was all the more exasperating because the excitement and agitation by the strength of which the Reform Bill was carried in the teeth of so much resistance were kept up by the working men."[5] "Rightly or wrongly they [the masses] believed their strength had been kept in reserve or *in terrorism* to secure the carrying of the Reform Bill, and that when it was carried they were immediately thrown over by those whom they had helped to pass it."[6] In short, the Reform Bill prevented a revolution; the middle class would have availed itself of the brute strength of the working class in order to have attained its end,—political power.[7] The Reform Bill admitted the middle class into political partnership with the aris-

[5] McCarthy, *A History of Our Own Times,* 1:110.

[6] *Ibid.,* 111.

[7] *Ibid.,* 108; also Gammage, *History of the Chartist Movement,* 3 *et seq.*

tocratic element which had hitherto enjoyed a political monopoly.[8] The middle class, "on the one hand, had taken advantage of the real wants of the classes below it, and of the social ideas which had been called into existence by the French Revolution; it had not scrupled to employ what cannot be regarded in any other light than as an unconstitutional pressure to bear upon Parliament. On the other hand, it had worked constitutionally by an alliance with one of the governing classes, namely the whigs."[9]

In the United States, thanks to the influence of the frontier, manhood suffrage became a reality. In England, the frontier element was lacking; the balance of power was different. The landed aristocracy was forced to admit the middle class into the monopoly of political authority; but at this point the two enfranchised interests combined to prevent further extension of political privileges. In the United States the alignment of interests in the struggle for the extension of the suffrage was between the educated and wealthy classes of the seaboard against the frontier and the wage earners.

The laboring classes of England felt that they had been tricked and used as a catspaw by the middle class; and as a consequence arose the Chartist movement. This was a wage-earners movement,[10] and was opposed by both the landlords, and the commercial and manufacturing class; it proved a failure. The English workers lacked the strong helping hand which the frontier extended to their American brothers; and the opposition

[8] The "reformed Commons" passed, in 1833, an act granting "£20,000 for the purposes of education,"—the beginning, in England, of national grants for education.

[9] Bright, J. F., *An History of England,* 3:1432. See also Flower, B. O., *How England averted a Revolution of Force.*

[10] Bright, J. F., *An History of England,* 4:86–7.

was more strongly entrenched. The Dorr war was the Chartist movement of Rhode Island; although nominally a failure, it was in reality a success. The Rhode Islanders were able to obtain a considerable extension of suffrage. In Rhode Island the land-owning class was not powerful; the barriers in the road toward the participation of the masses in political affairs were far less formidable than in England. In the latter one of the chief factors in the equation was the landlord class; in Rhode Island, this factor was almost negligible.

The fight for the repeal of the Corn Laws is interesting, for our purpose, chiefly because of the humanitarian aspects inseparably connected with it. Here humanitarian principles appear in an aspect somewhat different from that assumed in the United States; the setting is not the same. In England the humanitarian leaders themselves were animated by motives and ideals which were not harmonious. "The general restlessness was so intense among the reflecting Conservatives and among the reflecting Liberals; and those who looked to the past agreed with those who looked to the future, in energetic dissatisfaction with a sterile present. We need only to look around to recognize the unity of the original impulse which animated men who dreaded and hated each other, and inspired books that were as far apart as a humoristic novel and a treatise on the Sacrament."[11] In England we find the familiar type of humanitarian leaders who looked to the past, who were cast in a mould similar to that which furnished the humanitarian leaders of New England; but we also find a second type which is radically different, these men were looking ahead and belonged to an aggressive, rising class in the community. The presence of the second is explained by

[11] Morley, *Life of Cobden,* 1:90.

various students of English history. Morley writing of the forces back of the Anti-Corn Law League states: "The promptings of a commercial shrewdness were gradually enlarged into enthusiasm for a far-reaching principle, and the hard-headed man of business gradually felt himself touched with the generous glow of the patriot and the deliverer."[12] "The advocacy of free trade was not mere enthusiasm on the part of philanthropists who wished to see their own countrymen better off; for enthusiasm rarely influences a considerable percentage of society, even under the most favorable circumstances. . . . It was an accident, and a very important accident, that the advocates of free trade could point to natural justice, could dilate on the outrageous wrong of the system against which they arrayed themselves. . . ."[13]

The year 1850 found the middle and land-owning classes still in the saddle; manhood suffrage and tax-supported schools were reforms of the future. Six important points of difference between England and the United States during the period 1820–1850, may be mentioned. The existence of these differences, in view of the preceding discussion, offers a fairly satisfactory reason for the different trend of educational evolution in the two countries during this period. (a) The absence of sharp and rigid demarkation of classes, and of a landed aristocracy, in the United States. (b) The existence of the American frontier. (c) The existence, in England, of an established church whose influence was due in no small measure, if we may judge from American experience, to the absence of a frontier. (d) Considerable differentiation of nationalities and races in the United States. (e) The policy of national isolation pursued by

[12] *Ibid.*, 142; see also *ibid.*, 141.
[13] Rogers, *Cobden and Political Opinion*, 19.

the United States government. Such a policy undoubtedly had an important influence upon internal affairs.[14] (f) Early immigration into the United States consisted of the cream of the English middle class.

Soon after the suffrage was extended[15] in the latter years of the decade of the sixties, the act of 1870 was passed which made education compulsory, and made it optional with local school boards whether fees should be collected or not.[16] This long step forward in the history of English education is comparable with the rapid progress in Rhode Island during the latter part of the decade of the forties, after the extension of the suffrage. The resolution of the political and social forces acting in England during our period does not necessitate a restatement of the conditions, social, political and economic, which produced the tax-supported public school; but instead it tends to strengthen and confirm the opinion which was formed as a result of the study of industrial and educational evolution in the United States during the last three decades of the first half of the last century. After 1850, humanitarianism assumed, in England, a phase similar to that which has been considered in the United States. The workingmen changed their attitude somewhat; they deserted the individualism of earlier days and turned toward collectivist ideals. The Reform Act of 1867 and subsequent ones were fathered by a Conservative ministry, not one adhering to Liberal principles. The true basis of the alliance of Tories and working people "was their common dissent from individualistic liberalism."[17] "When young England came under

[14] Gumplowicz, *Sociologie et Politique,* sec. 27.
[15] Green, T. H., *Works,* 3:339. Previously cited.
[16] Casson and Whiteley, *The Education Act of 1902,* 23.
[17] Dicey, A. V., *Law and Public Opinion in England,* 251–52.

the guidance of Mr. Disraeli, Tories could afford at times to exhibit sentimental friendliness toward workmen engaged in conflict with manufacturers whose mills offended the aesthetic taste, and whose radicalism shook the political authority of benevolent aristocrats."[18]

[18] *Ibid.*, 242.

Appendix II
Biographical Notes[1]

HENRY BARNARD (1811–1900) descended from an old Hartford family. He graduated from Yale in 1830; and was admitted to the bar five years later. From 1837 to 1840, Dr. Barnard was a member of the Connecticut legislature. He was appointed, in 1838, secretary of the newly created Connecticut board of school commissioners, and served four years in that capacity. From 1843 to 1849, Dr. Barnard served as commissioner of schools of the state of Rhode Island; he was recalled to Connecticut in 1850 to become state superintendent of schools. He was president of the University of Wisconsin from 1857 to 1859; and was appointed first United States commissioner of education in 1867. This famous and indefatigable educational leader was the author of many books and articles upon educational topics; the editor of the *Connecticut Common School Journal* for eight years, of the *Rhode Island School Journal* from 1843 to 1849, and of *Barnard's American Journal of Education.*

ORESTES A. BROWNSON (1803–1876) was born in Stockbridge, Vermont. His father died while he was yet a small boy, leaving the family in poverty. The boy was cared for by elderly relatives who reared him in "a simple, precise and puritanical way." Mr. Brownson was educated in an academy at Ballston; he entered the universalist

[1] See section on "The Humanitarian Movement," ch. III.

ministry, but afterwards accepted the Roman Catholic faith. He was the author of several books, and was much interested in the projects of Robert Owen.

JAMES G. CARTER (1795–1849) was the son of a farmer. In 1820, he graduated from Harvard, and during the next ten years taught school at Leominster, Massachusetts. Mr Carter was the pioneer agitator of the educational movement of the period; he began the work for educational reform about 1823. As a member of the Massachusetts legislature he drafted the bill which established the famous Massachusetts Board of Education of which Horace Mann was the first secretary. Mr. Carter was appointed a member of this board.

WILLIAM ELLERY CHANNING (1780–1842), a clergyman, was the son of a lawyer, and the grandson of a signer of the Declaration of Independence. He graduated, with high honors, from Harvard. Mr. Channing was a unitarian and took an active part in the agitations for organized charity, temperance reform, education for workingmen, and the abolition of slavery.

JAMES FREEMAN CLARKE (1810–1888) was also a unitarian clergyman. He was the grandson of General William Hull and a cousin of Commodore Isaac Hull. Harvard College and Harvard Divinity School claim him as an alumnus.

RALPH WALDO EMERSON (1803–1882). "Eight generations of cultured, conscientious, and practical ministers preceded him." Harvard was also the *alma mater* of this famous philosopher and transcendentalist.

FREDERIC HENRY HEDGE (1805–1890), educator and minister, was the son of a teacher. He also graduated from Harvard.

SAMUEL LEWIS (1799–1854) was the first and only superintendent of common schools in Ohio. He came from old New England stock. His father was the captain of a coasting vessel; but in 1814 he gave up the sea-faring life and settled on an Ohio farm. Mr. Lewis was a lawyer; he was admitted to the bar in 1822.

HORACE MANN (1796–1859), the most famous of the educational leaders of the period, was a farmer boy. He graduated from Brown University in 1819, was admitted to the bar in 1823, was elected to the state legislature in 1827, became president of the state senate in 1836, was secretary of the Massachusetts Board of Education from 1837 to 1848, was elected to Congress in 1848, and was nominated, in 1852, governor of Massachusetts, but was defeated at the polls. At the time of his death, Mr. Mann was president of Antioch College, in Ohio. Horace Mann worked unceasingly in the cause of education, and undoubtedly hastened his death by his devotion to work of educational betterment. His reports as secretary of the Massachusetts Board of Education are educational classics.

THEODORE PARKER (1810–1860). The father of Mr. Parker was a federalist and a unitarian; his grandfather is said to have commanded the company of minute men that were fired upon by the British on April 19, 1775. He was a student at Harvard, and entered the ministry.

ROBERT RANTOUL, JR. (1805–1852) was a lawyer and a Harvard graduate. His father was a druggist, and was for some years a member of the state legislature. The father was much interested in reform movements. Robert, Junior, was a member of the state legislature, and later of the United States Congress. He was also a member of the first board of education in Massachusetts.

GEORGE RIPLEY (1802–1880) was the son of a prominent New England merchant and politician. He was a graduate of Harvard College and Harvard Divinity

School. Mr. Ripley was a student of philosophy, and one of the leaders in the Brook Farm experiment.

HENRY DAVID THOREAU (1817–1862). Thoreau's father was "bred to the mercantile line and continued in it until failure in business;" he then became a pencil maker. Mr. Thoreau graduated from Harvard in 1837.

Bibliography

I. CONTEMPORARY SOURCES

A. Documents and Reports

Massachusetts, Colonial Laws of. Reprinted, Boston, 1889.
Massachusetts, The Perpetual Laws of. 1801.
New York, Statutes of the State of. Albany, 1847.
Reports of the Census Bureau.
South Carolina, Statutes at Large of; edited by Thos. Cooper. Columbia, 1839.

B. Books and Pamphlets

Address to the Mechanics of the District of Columbia. Washington, 1835.
Carter, J. G., Schools of Massachusetts in 1820. Old South Leaflets.
Chickering, Jesse, On Population and Immigration. Boston, 1848.
Cooper, Thos., Elements of Political Economy. London, 1831.
Curry, Daniel, Metropolitan City of America. N. Y., 1853.
Cutler, Ephraim, Life and Times of. Cin. O., 1890.
Foote, J. P., Schools of Cincinnati. Cin. O., 1855.
Hammond, J. D., History of Political Parties in New York. Syracuse, 1852.
Hosack, David, Memoir of DeWitt Clinton. N. Y., 1829.
Jenkins, J. S., History of Political Parties in New York. Auburn, 1846.
Kay, Jos., The Social Condition and Education of the People. London, 1850.
Luther, Seth, An Address to the Working Men of New En-

gland, on the State of Education and on the Condition of the Producing Classes in Europe and America. Phila., 3 ed., 1836.

Mann, Horace, Education and Prosperity. Reprinted, Boston, 1904.

Mills, Robt., Statistics of Charleston. Charleston, 1826.

Pitkin, Thos., A Statistical View of the Commerce of the U. S. New Haven, 1835.

Proceedings of the Working Men's Convention. Boston, July 4, 1834.

Randall, S. S., Common School System of the State of N. Y. Troy, N. Y., 1851.

Rantoul, Robt. Jr., Memoirs. Boston, 1854.

Simpson, S. A., A Manual of Workingmen. Phila., 1831.

Skidmore, Thos., Rights of Man to Property. N. Y., 1829.

Thompson, Z., History of Vermont. Burlington, Vt., 1853.

Thornwell, J. H., Letters to Gov. Manning on Public Instruction in South Carolina. Charleston, 1853.

Tucker, Geo., Progress of the United States. N. Y., 1843.

Tudor, Wm., Letters of the Eastern States. Boston, 1821.

Wayland, F., Political Economy. N. Y., 1836.

Winterbotham, Wm., An Historical, Geographical and Philosophical View of the United States. London, 1795.

C. Newspapers and Periodicals

American Daily Advertiser. (Phila.)
American Journal of Education. (Boston.)
Baltimore Morning Chronicle.
Barnard's Journal of Education. (Hartford.)
Boston Courier.
Boston Gazette
Columbia Centinel. (Boston.)
Connecticut Common School Journal. (Hartford.)
The Craftsman. (Rochester.)
The Crisis. (London.)
De Bow's Review. (New Orleans.)
Delaware Free Press. (Wilmington.)
Farmers' and Mechanics' Journal. (Alexander, N. Y.)
Franklin Gazette. (Phila.)

Free Enquirer. (N. Y.)
Hazard's Register of Pennsylvania. (Phila.)
The Man. (N. Y.)
Mechanics Free Press. (Phila.)
National Intelligencer. (Washington.)
National Laborer. (Phil.)
New England Palladium and Commercial Advertiser. (Boston.)
New York Daily Sentinel.
New York Evening Post.
New York Morning Courier.
New York Mercury.
New York Spectator.
New York Tribune.
Niles' Register. (Baltimore.)
North American Review. (N. Y.)
Ohio School Journal.
Philadelphia Liberator.
Republican Star. (Easton, Md.)
Richmond Enquirer.
The Washingtonian. (Washington.)
Working Man's Advocate. (N. Y.)

II. RECENT LITERATURE

A. Documents and Reports

Reports of the Census Bureau.
Reports of the Commissioner of Education.
Report of the Treasury Department; Immigration. 1820–1903.
Rogers, E. H., Minority Report on Hours of Labor. Mass. House Bill, No. 4, 1867.

B. Books and Pamphlets

Adams, Francis, The Free School System of the U. S. London, 1875.
Bacon, L. W., A History of American Christianity. N. Y., 1900.

Bourne, W. O., History of Public School Society. N. Y., 1870.
Bright, J. F., A History of England. London, 1877.
Bruce, P. A., Economic History of Virginia in the Seventeenth Century. N. Y., 1896.
Bruce, P. A., History of North America, Vol. 17; Rise of the New South. Phila., 1905.
Casson and Whiteley, The Education Act of 1902. London, 1903.
Chase, Benj., History of old Chester. Auburn, N. H., 1869.
Cobb, S. H., The Rise of Religious Liberty in America. N. Y., 1902.
Courtenay, W. A., Education in South Carolina. Charleston, 1881.
De Forest, H. P., History of Westborough. Westborough, 1891.
Desmond, H. J., The Know-Nothing Party. Washington, 1905.
Dexter, E. G., History of Education in the U. S. N. Y., 1904.
Dicey, A. V., Law and Public Opinion in England. N. Y., 1905.
Dorchester, D., Christianity in the U. S. N. Y., 1888.
Draper, A. S., Origin and Development of the N. Y. Common School System. Syracuse, 1903.
Dunning, W. A., Political Theories from Luther to Montesquieu. N. Y., 1905.
Edmonds, F. S., History of the Central High School of Philadelphia. Phila., 1902.
Ely, R. T., The Labor Movement in America. N. Y., 1886.
Fiske, John, The Beginnings of New England. Boston, 1889.
Fiske, John, The Dutch and Quaker Colonies in America. Boston, 1899.
Fiske, John, Old Virginia and her Neighbors. Boston, 1897.
Flower, B. O., How England Averted a Revolution of Force. Trenton, N. J.
Frothingham, O. B., Transcendentalism in New England. N. Y., 1876.
Gammage, R., History of the Chartist Movement. London, 1894.
Green, T. H., Works. London, 1890.
Greene, M. L., The Development of Religious Liberty in Connecticut. Boston, 1905.
Gumplowicz, L., Sociologie et Politique. Paris, 1898.

Hinsdale, B. A., Horace Mann. N. Y., 1898.
Hobhouse, L. T., Democracy and Reaction. London, 1904.
Hobson, J. A., Economics of Distribution. N. Y., 1900.
Jenkins, H. M., Pennsylvania, Colonial and Federal. Phila., 1903.
King, Rufus, Ohio. Boston, 1888.
Kuhns, O., German and Swiss Settlements in Pennsylvania. N. Y., 1901.
Leach, A. F., English Schools at the Time of the Reformation. London, 1896.
Lossing, B. J., The Empire State. Hartford, 1888.
McCall, S. W., Life of Thaddeus Stevens. Boston, 1899.
McCarthy, J., A History of Our Own Times. London, 1882.
McMaster, J. B., Acquisition of Political, Social and Industrial Rights. Cleveland, 1903.
McMaster, J. B., History of the People of the U. S. N. Y., 1884–1900.
Martin, G. H., Evolution of the Massachusetts Public School System. Boston, 1893.
Mathews, A., Ohio and her Western Reserve. N. Y., 1902.
Morley, John, Life of Cobden. Boston, 1881.
Mowry, A. M., The Dorr War. Providence, 1901.
Myers, G., History of Tammany Hall. N. Y., 1901.
Nieboer, H. J., Slavery as an Industrial System. The Hague, 1900.
Orth, S. P., Centralization of Administration in Ohio. Columbia Studies, Vol. 16, 1903.
Palmer, A. E., The New York Public School. N. Y., 1905.
Patten, S. N., Development of English Thought. N. Y., 1899.
Perrin, J. W., Compulsory Education, University of Chicago, 1896.
Powell, L. P., History of Education in Delaware. Washington, 1893.
Rann, W. S., History of Chittenden County (Vermont). Syracuse, N. Y., 1886.
Richman, I. B., Rhode Island. N. Y., 1902.
Riddle, Wm., School History of Lancaster (Penn.). Lancaster, 1905.
Ritchie, D. G., Natural Rights. London, 1895.

Rogers, J. E. T., Cobden and Modern Public Opinion. London, 1873.

Schafer, Jos., Origin of the System of Land Grants for Education. Bulletin of the University of Wisconsin, 1902.

Secomb, D. F., History of Amherst (N. H.). Concord, N. H., 1883.

Sewall, S., History of Woburn. Boston, 1868.

Simonds, J. C., The Story of Labor in All Ages. Chicago, 1886.

Simons, A. M., Class Struggles in America. Chicago, 1905.

Smith, C. L., History of Education in North Carolina. Washington, 1888.

Smith and Rann, History of Rutland County (Vt.). Syracuse, N. Y., 1886.

Stanwood, Edw., American Tariff Controvercies [*sic*] in the Nineteenth Century. Boston, 1903.

Steiner, B. C., History of Education in Maryland. Washington, 1894.

Stevenson, R. T., History of North America, Vol. 12; The Growth of the Nation. Phila., 1905.

Tiffany, F., Charles Francis Barnard, His Life and Work. Boston, 1895.

Venable, W. H., Literary Culture in the Ohio Valley. Cin., 1891.

Webb, S. and B., Industrial Democracy. London, 1902.

Weeden, W. B., Economic and Social History of New England. Boston, 1890.

Wickersham, J. P., History of Education in Pennsylvania. Lancaster, Penn., 1886.

C. Articles

Andrews, J. B., Employer's Associations. In *The Commons* June, 1905.

Blackmar, F. W., History of Suffrage in Legislation in the U. S. In *The Chautauquan,* Oct., 1895.

Carlton, F. T., The Home and the School. In *Education,* Dec., 1905.

Carlton, F. T., The Influence of Recent Economic and Social Changes upon Educational Aims, Ideals and Methods. In *Journal of Pedagogy,* March, 1906.

Carlton, F. T., The Industrial Value of Manual Training. In *Engineering Magazine,* Sept., 1904.

Carlton, F. T., The South During the Last Decade. In *Sewanee Review,* April, 1904.

Carlton, F. T., Humanitarianism, Past and Present. In *The International Journal of Ethics,* Oct., 1906.

Carlton, F. T., The Workingmen's Party of New York City, 1829–1831. In *The Political Science Quarterly,* Sept., 1907.

Channing, Edw., The Narragansett Planters. In *Johns Hopkins University Studies,* 1886.

Hinsdale, Mary, A Legislative History of the Public School System of the State of Ohio. In *Report of Commissioner of Education,* 1901.

Hubbard, Elbert, Slaughter of the Innocents. In *American Federationist,* April, 1905.

Mayo, A. D., Development of the Common School System. In *Reports of the Commissioner of Education.*

Robinson, M. H., History of Taxation in New Hampshire. In *American Economic Association Publications,* 1902.

Simons, A. M., The Rise of Labor in America. In *International Socialist Review,* Sept., 1904.

Simons, M. W., Education in the South. In *American Journal of Sociology,* Nov., 1904.

Turner, F. J., Colonization of the West. In *American Historical Review,* Jan., 1906.

Turner, F. J., The Significance of the Frontier in American History. In *Reports of American Historical Association,* 1893.